The Revd Dr Donna J. Lazenby is
of St Mellitus College, South V
Spirituality and Apologetics. She i:
Transcendence and Immanence in tne vvorks oj virginia vvooj una ...
Murdoch (Bloomsbury, 2014). Donna's PhD won the John Templeton
Award for Theological Promise 2011. Alongside lecturing and tutor-
ing, she continues to exercise her priestly ministry as Lead Minister
of The Hayes Church, Kenley.

To encourage the prophets

DIVINE SPARKS

Everyday encounters with
God's incoming kingdom

Donna Lazenby

First published in Great Britain in 2017

Society for Promoting Christian Knowledge
36 Causton Street
London SW1P 4ST
www.spck.org.uk

British Library Cataloguing-in-Publication Data
A catalogue record for this book is available from the British Library

ISBN 978–0–281–07494–5
eBook ISBN 978–0–281–07945–2

Typeset by Manila Typesetting Company
First printed in Great Britain by Ashford Colour Press
Subsequently digitally printed in Great Britain

eBook by Manila Typesetting Company

Produced on paper from sustainable forests

For prophecy and contemplative vision, of which prophecy is a by-product, depend upon the positioning of the Church at the overlap of the ages (see 1 Corinthians 10.11). As Charles Péguy wrote: 'Everything depends upon that dovetailing of the temporal and the eternal. Everything collapses once that adjustment is unsettled, or out of true, or taken to pieces.' The sun then goes down on the prophets; vision fades; the eyes close, or become glazed over.

Kenneth Leech, *Prayer and Prophecy*[1]

To say that there is an absolute difference in being between God and the world is to say: look out, up even, not in or down, if you want to know the real source of our being and meaning. To look into the self or the earth is to put your trust in that which cannot save. The doctrine of the Trinity is the Church's resource against idolatry, against worshipping anything other than the one who by the eternal Spirit raised Jesus from the dead . . . There is no God within, but there is the Son who comes alongside us in mercy and judgement. There is no God in the earth, but there is the Spirit who comes, through that same Son, to transform our personal being into that which it was created for, a living sacrifice of praise and thanks to God the Father.

Colin Gunton, *Father, Son and Holy Spirit*[2]

I have tried to suggest to the modern Christian how close the connection is between the great doctrines of his religion and that 'inner life' which is too often regarded as a more spiritual alternative to orthodoxy: how rich and splendid is the Christian account of reality, and how much food it has to offer to the contemplative soul.

Evelyn Underhill, *The School of Charity*[3]

The work of the Spirit is related to the creation's cohesion and destiny in Christ, but his distinct function is at once to restore lost order and . . . transformation into the conditions of the age to come. This does not happen in a general way, but takes place as particular parts of the creation are set free through Christ and enabled to be themselves, and so anticipations of the universal redemption in the age to come.

Colin Gunton, *Theology through the Theologians*[4]

Contents

Contents

Introduction
The need for prophecy

I am, first of all, a woman attempting to learn how faithfully to follow Jesus Christ. I am also a priest in the Church of England, a teacher of theology, and an inhabitant of this contemporary culture in which we 'live and move and have our being'.[5] And, while living these callings, I have begun to develop several key convictions.

First, the world around us, for all that it claims to be 'secular', has largely stolen the claims of the gospel and attempts to 'sell' us gospel-shaped promises which only the gospel itself can actually promise and satisfy. We see this in advertising, but also in all kinds of commercial-speak, promotional material, multimedia correspondence and on so many surfaces within our image-obsessed postmodern society which tries to suggest to us the meaning of our lives while exploiting our most intimate desires and stimulating them to the tune of false offerings. It is the 'age-defying' face cream that promises eternal life; the internet provider who can grant us 'infinity'; the mobile phone company that will extend 'endless power' to its customers; the make-up brand that grants beautification by 'the Spirit' or a mascara called 'Resurrection'.

What this, itself, reveals is that the contemporary, allegedly 'secular' culture of the early twenty-first-century UK[6] is filled to the brim with yearning: and with gospel-shaped yearning in particular (as the following reflections show).

And this means that the Church is in desperate need of prophets today: of a recovery, a renewal, in the gifting of prophecy. We need prophets who can reveal the lies and false-selling, dispel the untruths and reveal the God who is *actually* the life longed and sought for. This is *true*, biblical, prophecy: not a magical foretelling of otherwise unknown and unpredictable events, but the gift of people who, from the midst of their culture, are able to speak to that culture of its relationship to God, and to render to God in prayer the predicaments and transfigurations of the culture. We need prophets who can spot, with eyes tuned to double vision, the yearnings of the culture as they appear in the promises of advertisers and companies and other so-called 'secular' agendas, who can then help the culture interpret these longings – come to some conscious interpretation of its own desires – and, crucially, not leave its inhabitants with nothing but empty promises with which to shape their lives, but direct these hearts and bodies and souls to their true source and end.

This is a work of the Spirit, and it is truly spiritual, *charismatic* work: not in some gnostic or secularized airy-fairy sense, but in the real, gritty, wholesome, agitating, transforming sense with which the Spirit of God revealed in the life of the Trinity heaves up, shakes up, reorders and makes brilliant our beauty-bound lives. Much of the world is still hung in crucifixion: 'stuck' on the first side of the cross, protesting the agony of its alienation from its meaning and calling and purpose. This is a profound loneliness. The work of the Spirit of God is to press creation through the cross and out to the other side, the side defined by the fact and promise of resurrection. Ultimately, this is God's work, wrought by divine action. But we creatures, called ourselves to be *redeemed* creatures and *priests* who embrace our kindred creation and remind her of her home, have our part to play: and now is the time for a new age of prophecy.

Personally, when it comes to discerning the nature, meaning and value of faith I do not think that the greatest difficulty for our culture is atheism, or nihilism. In my daily round of missional and pastoral duties as a priest, I meet very few actual atheists or nihilists. To engage at all in the forward trajectory of our lives, to make plans and enjoy ourselves, to create families and friendships, to try to find our 'true identity', to dream dreams and make adventures, and strive for various fulfilments, is to state that we believe life to be meaningful, purposeful, worthwhile, even if we are unaware of how to ground the value (or don't tend to think about it). As I say, I meet very few atheists or nihilists – if any. Who I *do* meet are the many people – inquisitive, open, searching, wondering, uncertain, grateful, doubting, tender, questing, hopeful, devoted, miraculous – whose lives are full of yearnings they cannot name, desires they know not how to interpret, haunting instincts of a missing 'centre' and the possibility of a wholeness not yet glimpsed but persistently present and longed for. How else could advertising get the grip it does on us? Meanwhile, their value-convictions are largely gospel-shaped: the vulnerable are not to be cast off, but protected; self-sacrifice is the most meaning-charged expression of love and has power to enchant us; 'life after death' is very possible. The struggle for our culture is not atheism or nihilism: it is *amnesia*, the basic having forgotten from where these convictions came, an inability therefore to know how to 'name' them and a disorientation with regard to how to pursue them. Again: how else the ability of advertising to attempt to sell gospel-shaped promises in particular?

In this missionary situation the Church needs prophets who, like Paul in Athens, can walk around in the culture, listen to it, look at it, help it to see what it worships and where it needs to reorient its vision if it is to pursue its questions with any hope of finding answers. The Church needs prophets who engage the double vision of kingdom and culture, bringing the two into conversational traction: prophets who, as witnesses to the gospel of Jesus Christ, are announcing the good news afresh to dispel the amnesia.

This is a call to every follower of Jesus Christ: to develop our prophetic vision in order to see how the world's aching and longing for God's transformation sits within the pregnancy of the Spirit's brooding presence: that Spirit who brings God's promised future into the immediate present. 'The Spirit and the bride say, "Come"' (Revelation 22.17). It is possible to see God everywhere: or almost everywhere, and certainly every day. We can learn to become aware of the ways in which he is pressing into the world he has made and loves, rather as a child nestles into a parent in the early hours of the morning.

Finally, an encouragement to the Church: strangely, the world often shows more confidence in the power of the gospel to win hearts than we do. The simple fact that so much advertising, so many of the surfaces of our society, are covered with gospel-shaped cravings should encourage the Church to realize the timeliness of the message she has to proclaim. The founder of the Salvation Army, William Booth, when asked about the particular and fresh valuing of music in that movement, is reputed to have answered, 'Why should the devil have all the best tunes?' I am tempted, when looking at our culture, to add, 'And why should he have ours?'

The following reflections are designed to help you develop prophetic vision. In each I share with you my own observation of the work of the Spirit in an everyday situation: whether this is to foreground the agonized protest of a landscape that is yearning for its redemption, or to celebrate an occasion of the Spirit's redeeming presence bursting through, bringing freedom and life. Each reflection ends with 'Questions for reflection' designed to stimulate your vision and thinking about comparable observations that can be made in your own daily life. The reflections can be read, mulled and discussed either with friends (perhaps taking one a week) or alone, in a meditative spirit.

My hope is that, engaging with these reflections and the questions following them, you will not be left unchanged, but will discover that you are developing and strengthening your own prophetic vision, so that, called upon to dispel the lies of exploitative media and to lead God's creatures to living water, you will contribute to nothing less than the coming of God's kingdom.

Frozen

Acts 8.26–35

On a recent visit to our local primary school I noticed a new set of beautifully painted inscriptions written on the walls. They are pieces of motivation, teaching and advice, designed to inspire the children, to form their character, to give purpose to their learning: wisdom from Harry Potter is scrawled in black, encouraging the discovery of an inherent power for living.

But the inheritance of the idea is clear: it is gospel-shaped. Moreover, five minutes glancing at life (and guessing at the lives these young people have yet to live) reveals that the real anchoring and satisfaction of these promises *needs* the gospel. In our allegedly secular classrooms, the promises of the gospel remain, glistening through the words and pictures we use to help our youngest find their life's direction. These promises of the classroom cannot, of course, deliver what they offer: they claim what only the gospel possesses – and gives.

One spectacular contemporary example of gospel-encrypted film is Disney's *Frozen*. While framed in the genre of fairy tale, its narrative enchants all ages with a hauntingly familiar shape . . .

*   *   *

It is sometimes alleged that our culture has divested itself of its Christian heritage, and has entered a 'post-Christian', even secular, phase (as if to mark the passing of a civilization, we are asked to speak of inhabiting 'post-Christendom'). But inspection of the same cultural consciousness reveals an imagination still captivated by Jesus: though there is hesitation to speak his name.

Christian ideas have far from disappeared from the cultural imagination, but are discovered firmly embedded (though with a distinctive unknowing enshrined) in legal, educational and moral systems

1

which we persistently applaud and defend; and, indeed, in forms of entertainment that reach out to tussle and grasp the essentials of human living.

Despite a surface-level cultural amnesia concerning the origins of our best and enduring convictions – concerning the inviolable status of honour, sacrifice, love, family, friendship, duty, progress in identity, service, community, dignity – convictions which have new parents speeding back to Church for the formation of their children; despite this surface self-forgetfulness, the subterranean levels of the collective cultural consciousness bulge rich with the bounty of hidden treasures.

Periodically, these treasures surface in crystallized paradigms, offering back to the library of life especially refined instalments of the narratives that shape our deepest meaning, through tales that carve our souls from earliest learning. These are not so much new devices as erupting shafts of those granites and basalts that gird our foundations, as any excavation will show, and they come up glistening: these persisting gospel values.

One sure storehouse of Christian theology is the world of Hollywood and Disney: and it is interesting to observe that as the repository of publically offered Christian monumentality is repressed, the enchanted worlds presented by Disney and Hollywood only gain influence and definition: as what is oppressed in one place, being indissolubly essential to the substance, simply erupts to the surface elsewhere. Upon our private and public screens themes of redemption, forgiveness, reconciliation, self-sacrifice, atoning love thrive and proliferate. At the heart of the recent craze – craved as much by adults as by children, so starved are we of material for maturing in the Spirit – is Christ himself (again), as the suffering and self-offering of an unsung hero(ine) holds the centre of Disney's recent (re-)creation: *Frozen*.

This film calls on themes of identity, natural and supernatural gifting, power, renewal (personal and ecological), friendship and discipleship: and redemption made possible through one act of self-giving, an act of 'true love' which is alone capable of breaking the spell that

2

holds creation and human relationships in thrall to life-numbing powers. It is an act of self-giving, which in a discrete moment unlocks the logic of deathliness, thereby equipping a spirit to move out and thaw the whole world.

Everywhere in this story is the gospel encrypted.

Frozen is a tale of two sisters, Elsa and Anna. Elsa is the Snow Queen and everything she touches freezes. The safety and freedom of her world appears to require her self-incarceration: but in this process of imprisonment it is Elsa's own heart that we watch slowly freezing, while her rejection of her self, her sister Anna and her community sends creation into a corresponding deathly deep freeze. Distortions and corruptions in the human heart and mind plunge the world around to sub-zero.

Elsa causes a huge amount of trouble and destruction and disorder in the film. But she is not evil: she is a person trying to work it all out alone, outside any relation (sin). She is a person trying to live without relationship, without community, without love: bounded by the close of her imaginative circuit; without faith that a greater wisdom than her own might provide a better pattern to live by; without hope for the healing of past pains and rejections and mistaken identifications; without the awareness that community waits to love her, accept her, help her.

Consequently, propensities in Elsa's character – actually neutral in themselves (as the making of splendid ice rinks finally testifies) – lacking guidance beyond her own limited perspective become uncontrollable sources of power*lessness*, of obsessions and neuroses. The mark of Elsa's self-conceived freedom, her flight, is a race into solitary imprisonment. She flees from community: and in her wake, all land – trees, lakes, flowers – are locked solid, un-breathing, cast into an 'eternal winter', as little Anna has the daring to tell her. Creation suffers the brokenness of the human heart. Sin – living a life in exile, at a distance from wisdom, from life – sets nothing and no one free, but binds hearts, minds and imaginations, and petrifies the political, social and natural world into a dulled-down system of status-quo living. Elsa believes the disconnection constitutes her happiness: but this is only numbness, the anaesthetizing of particular questions (as, indeed, she sings, cursing her own foolishness: 'I can't be free – from the storm within. There's so much fear . . .'). Who am I, *really*? How do I live with others? How do I relate to others? What am I to do with who I really am? If I'm honest about myself, who can love me? *Am* I loved? Can I be truly freed to be me, to discover who I am and who others are, not merely to live this wild unguided freedom which is actually a repression, a personal deep freeze? Can there be a thaw?

Elsa has not the spell for her own breaking.

But love is in pursuit.

Elsa's little sister, Anna, the weaker 'underdog' who, significantly, owns no magical powers, arrives with one vital quality: a reckless, prodigal refusal to give up the possibility of relationship with the sister who, from earliest memory, has always been pushing her away. So she comes running: she is God going after the lost sheep; she is God in pursuit of his covenant people, loving them to the ends of the earth (or where we may be more likely to find ourselves, stranded up the ice mountain of self-exile, creation-exile, other-exile); she is God arriving as we write ourselves off to Void; she is God come as much to free creation as the human being locked up at its centre.

In her flight from life, Elsa's consummative act of anticipated destruction is to plant a shard of ice in the pursuant's heart: one that will gradually turn little Anna to ice (everyone's dust-dealt destiny pre-Christ, we might add). The only known antidote to this outcome is an act of true love: and loyal to the law of fairy tale, this is interpreted by Anna to mean 'true love's kiss'. But in a moment of choosing – her own life, or her sister's (recalling Christ's own Gethsemane decision to pray return to the Father or to save the world)? – Anna turns from the lover's timely embrace to let fall on herself a blade about to kill her sister. The prodigal Anna – giving herself to the point of reckless ruin – freezes over entirely and is suspended in death. But in a recognizable moment of curious mingling, where the moment of self-sacrificing death is revealed as the simultaneous moment of death-defeating love, Anna's act of love – now revealed to dwell not in 'true love's kiss' after all but in the act of self-outpouring – reverses the system and thaws her to life. Anna is resurrected by love. The sacrament was in the giving. And Snow Queen Elsa is resurrected also, as, witnessing her sister's unrelenting self-giving, she is *recalled to* the existence of something with the power to reorient her nature: 'Love! Love, of course!' she cries, and in that moment creation begins to thaw into sparkling vivid colour (resonant, of course, of the renewed creation), as Elsa casts out sparkling rinks for the *community* to dance upon.

Fairy tales are not (just) for children. They capture in symbolic forms the deepest yearnings and questings of human hearts: hearts that live at the centre of an often incomprehensible, mysterious universe. And here is our culture finding a way to talk about enshrined ideas and beliefs. Nervous of applying Christian clothing to this tale, we find other ways to make manifest our belief in the redemptive power of self-sacrificing love. The film makes magic and enchantment its declared subject: but the film reveals that, like our culture, it is *itself* enchanted and captivated by an idea that won't go away; the idea of something whose name is Love being the solution to death, unlocking a creation otherwise held in thrall to deathly powers. Here is our culture musing over the cherished inheritance of the concept of self-sacrificing love as the key to unlock a new future – dwelling with it, working with it, renewing it, turning it over for inspection, wondering about it, incarnating it: feeling its power to win us again.

Meanwhile, some clever self-subversions are noteworthy too. The stereotypical staple of fairy tales, the charming Prince, is revealed as a wolf in sheep's clothing, a dangerously seductive chimera appearing as an angel of light. Furthermore (in significant connection?) the usually all-powerful symbol of 'true love's kiss' is revealed as anaemic, a romantic consolation, and nowhere near capable of saving the day: nowhere near roadworthy enough, tough enough, relentless enough to grasp and turn what is present invisibly in (and lurking just behind) the gesturing struggles of death and life taking place in the centre of the picture. Disney overturns its own false ideals. But there's an irony here, because it overturns these ideals while leaving untouched, at an ever-deeper underground level of freezing, the unlocked potential of the Real story that sources all its treasured symbols and makes of even its most beautiful films but a glass to be seen through darkly.

At the reconciliatory close of the film, as Anna speaks to Elsa, 'It's so good to have the [kingdom's] gates open', and Elsa responds, 'And they'll never be closed again', the film seems poignantly unconscious of the good news it is now expressing in imagery worthy of the book of Revelation.

For all its icy imagery, what *Frozen* reveals is what lies like a locked-up memory in the packed ice of our contemporary culture. Here are scattered fragments of historical papers reporting the existence of a man called Jesus of Nazareth. Here is also our haunting conviction (known in our bones but grown from where?) that 'winning' – what is most worth achieving, 'salvation' – arrives most perfectly in an unexpected form of seeming weakness. (We worship the underdog.) This love pours itself out with that mysteriously authoritative self-giving which outwits, and outshines, earthly powerhouses. We simply know, in our bones, to admire it. And each time it arrives, in slightly differing dress, the tale enchants our hearts afresh with the only power that is truly power: the love that thaws the way home, so that we might – in fact, not only in fiction – live happily ever after.

Questions for reflection

1   Which recent films have you seen, or stories have you read, that use gospel themes? What does this suggest about the enduring power of particular gospel values in your culture? What 'pictures of reality' are people being offered to live with? How are they being taught to interpret their desires?

2   Remember – call to mind – the fairy tales, myths or legends that captivated your heart as a child. What might their power to captivate you reveal about the deepest questions of your heart? What is your life's 'quest'?

3   What do the fairy tales current in our culture teach young people (and older!) about what they ought to desire, and about what is possible for them?

4   In *Frozen*, the anaemic and heavily romanticized 'true love's kiss' is traded away for a painful act of real cost. How does the traction of the cross speak to the forms of 'love' related in popular culture?

5   Our allegedly secular culture remains deeply enchanted by the life of Jesus, albeit often at underground levels. How confident

are you and your community about sharing Jesus' story? Is our 'unchurched' culture sometimes more captivated by our story than we are?

6 How do we, as people called to witness to Jesus, help others not to be left with fairy tales in place of truth? How can we unlock the gospel so it is seen not just as a 'fairy tale' but as describing and unlocking 'reality'?

A prayer for today

Lord, we pray for a thaw in our culture. The world is often confident to sing your song, as if it had imagined its own wisdom. Help your Church to melt the frozen layers of our culture where the memory of your Son's earthly life still lives, so that our society can celebrate again the remembered One who arrives to unlock the promised future. Amen.

Everyone wants to be rescued. People's disillusionment with life is that they cannot see that this is possible.

But are we yearning for the wrong kind of "rescuer"? The weak romantic kind? Are we asking the wrong questions? What we really need is so much more powerful.

Tattoo

Acts 17.16–34

Have you noticed that tattoos are back?

Our culture is often criticized for being overly superficial in its obsession with 'appearances', but I can't help relishing (rightly or wrongly!) the delight that many people are taking in bringing their bodies to express themselves in motifs and emblems. Self-expression is arriving on the body, is being etched in flesh.

Granted, the method of tattooing may be controversial for its violence on skin. But I wonder: do those of us who gaze on a God-in-flesh have something to *learn* from the tattoo-bearer's conviction that our fleshed selves speak as much about us as our thoughts and desires, have their part in the stating of our identity? As if our bodies were an extended canvas stretching out from the anchor of our hearts, ready and waiting to bear signs of our commitments? If Jesus is God as human flesh, if the incarnation makes its mark on this material, *all* material, ought we to care how our bodies speak?

If God's prophets are called to see and read 'the writing on the walls', to notice where God is speaking through the culture, then what are our fellows' bodies saying? Let's take a look . . .

*   *   *

Tattoos are back – these days in shops and streets and cafes and bars the arms of men and women are claimed: with shock-block armour, or an intricately woven wreath, patterns diving down long limbs to flourish at a broad or narrow ending. On some flesh canvases the inks lie cubic, heavy lines drawn straight, and broadly graven; on other frame-stretched weaves, on hair that plaits a finer matting, pinks and mauves and blues and greys paint jewel-like hues within fine-twisting lines. One marks a hunter-warrior. The other is elfin-Romantic and spells of princess dreams. Either way: the arm bears personal calligraphy, my body telling out for itself some significance at the heart of me, some thing I'd have you know: my daughter's name and her birthdate; a life-guiding quotation; an aspiration; an armour plate; an accolade; mythical fighter; soldier-spirit . . .

I'm on the train, and there, across the arm of the stranger opposite me, spreads a recognized symbol: an anchor with a heart, and above it in lilting letters a reference to Scripture, that subversive life-spring code.

I'm walking down the road, and a couple approaching me have bodies penned to show how opposites in spirit-life attracted. This ethereal fairy-creature: pen-stroked hair weaves round her elfin form while, up and down on arms and legs, subtle lights make bright in light-ning pastels wings and petals and blessing leaves. Beside her a pirate, or a freedom fighter, ink-dressed with gun and blade. While her tendril-lines speak lusting for enchantment, his heavy lines tell fury.

I'm in a restaurant and our waitress (who can't be over 20) on her inside wrists has penned to permanence 'No Lies', 'But Truth': she hates it now, she tells me, this tattoo, but adds it meant a lot to do. I won-der what the wrists needed to know, those delicate veils of life-well branches, appearing through in nature's bluey inks like ancient murals, deep invested. Crime to paint them over? These paints we each inherit, nature's writings, marking as earth-signs this world's forgotten mar-riage, heaven's first commitment to flesh, to which the watchful Spirit witnesses. Perhaps she didn't know that. Perhaps she despaired.

I notice that we choose to score in matter that which matters: flesh-encoding with instinct to incarnation what of our spirit we would have you know. These tender emblems – for whatever the message, the engraving's in frail flesh – are evocations, deep imprints of some heavy love, or loved thing heavily longed for. What is yours? What would you set as seal upon your arm? What seal as certain sign in your flesh etching?

'Expectant and watchful for the signs of God's presence' is our calling here, 'as he reveals his kingdom among us'.[7] So what's in flesh stirring? Here, in these tattoos, are signs and wonders surfacing as the heart-dream of the lion's life, or the cherishing of the enchanted sprite, or the celebration of lovers' fruits, or the promise made to one's own soul and written on the lifelines: finds the light – this speaking out where flesh meets air. Our bodies are writing out, expressing fleshly, our most important meanings. Are we reading?

And this is not the ghost-peeled-off of pagan thinking, which abandons our bodies to dust as spirit alone finds hope of resurrection life. No. The resurrection raised just this: this body, this flesh. So, rather, see here, our bodies *themselves* are speaking, as *flesh seeks hope*: these bodies spelling out our dreams, catching at identity, wreathing out in ink the lines of narratives, gestures to fantasy:

> that *what* will catch, though?
> for here's a call to recognize how this flesh-world makes out her meaning, springs her well of earth-erupted signs.
> And do we hear her cry?
> Do we recognize the world's self-painting?
> Do we know the canvases – each one for which he died – as speaking out the hope for saving as the questions, hot-pulsed, rise to life, shaping out the Way to earth-found wells?

*

I've been shopping all afternoon, and it's late, so I take the lift up through the car park. As we soar upwards the lift shakes worryingly, and we begin to doubt our direction.

'Which way are we going? Towards heaven?' one asks.

Another answers, 'Too soon for that just yet': his earth-hopes out.

The first pursues as the lift still shudders upwards, 'Ah yes, too early yet for going up *there*.'

Postmodern Man this time replies, 'If there is such a place at all,' his wan tone haunting, hopeless: not decisive, just suspended.

And I'm struck – we need a new Sistine, new ways of painting to the stars, to canvas heaven, for she was never 'up'.

We need new ink: to calligraph new hemispheres, and calibrate new pens and paint and words to show celestial, once again, on mortal frames, and in these terms, what's breathed by Immortality: which is to shape the cloud for brilliance's bursting.

Our art, as prophets, is sculpture: bending out the words and paint and ink to show the life that lies between the lines – the source of making.

The flesh is there: the arc's above us bending.

But this is crucial: how to paint the stars for a New Dawning? For that is what is needed now: new ways of speaking it all out that are meaningful for flesh and spirit. How to paint flesh pains, and the Word's response, his death-rewriting, Light-gulp shading? How to give word to the struggle, and indicate heavenly mending, precisely *as* flesh-blending? Where are the artists? Those who know how to give expression as spirit-in-form to what comes as in-spiration?

Grace, come and raise our nature – in your way, that's stroking flesh:

For you tell the lions to drop their growl and take their crowns;

For you ask the fairy Queen to abandon the season's ephemeral hues and braid her hair with everlasting garlands.

Our markings *then* are mysteries *now*. But one's thing sure. This body will rise. The author has written it.

Questions for reflection

1 In what ways do we 'mark' our bodies with meaning?

2 Where, in our culture, do you notice people attempting self-expression? What can we learn from this?

3 Where can we recognize 'signs of God's presence' – for which we are to be expectant and watchful – in the ways we treat our bodies? What yearnings, desires, assumptions and hopes are revealed in the way your culture treats the body?

4 What does it mean to you that physical resurrection (an embodied, corporeal future) is part of the promise of the gospel?

11

I find this gospel - that we will be resurrected bodily - quite Tattoo *confusing. How will this happen? What will we look like?*

Given this promise of physical resurrection, and the significance of the incarnation (God becoming flesh), what do you think followers of Jesus Christ should be saying (and showing) to our culture about the body, and the use and meaning of flesh? How could we start this conversation? *It could follow that it doesn't matter what we do to our bodies now because we will get a new one,*

No - 5 Do you think we need a new, or particular, language to speak of God? What are the challenges to language when it comes to speaking of God? How do *you* speak of him? What are the strengths and weaknesses of your own mode of articulation?

A prayer for today

Lord, you have created us as incarnate beings, through your Son: the principle of our immanence. Give us the eyes to see where both the assumptions of our culture and the in-breaking of your kingdom make their mark – and claim – on the body.

Teach us to relate to our bodies as creatures destined to rise: teach us what this means.

And empower us, by your Spirit, to love a world that reveals so much of its need in the body's aching. Amen.

12

Chasing loves: I am thirsty
John 4.1–26
John 7.37–39

So many of us are searching, hungering, and willing to make devastating moves that rewrite our lives at the mere hint that we might thereby discover 'happiness'.

In my work as a priest I meet many people who are leaving, or have been left by, their marriage partners. Wondering why this is – and what it means about the human heart – I am coming to take seriously the challenge to the human person in the midlife crisis because the reason for leaving is less often a case of a 'bad' marriage, or an irredeemably unpleasant partner, and more often a case of the spiritual pain of unfulfilled dreams and an insatiable sense of longing that calls the searching soul on from settled scenes. We cannot settle down. Perhaps – on some vital level – we aren't meant to.

We are deeply hungry. And a culture without ways of speaking of God both strives to make the wrong objects – people, things, dreams – satisfy our infinite needs (idols) and is condemned to have no language for beginning to articulate the crisis.

Reflecting on all this, I find myself wondering about the woman whom Jesus meets at the well (John 4). We may reflect often in our churches on what Jesus gives to her: but what does she come with? What state is she in when she comes to that well? Here is a woman who has had many lovers, coming alone to find water in deserts. In a world that has so downplayed and failed to explore the power of a woman's sexuality – the heat of her desires – what does Christ the lover of our souls have to say to our midlife crisis hours? Whatever those desires may be?

*   *   *

I wonder what she's searching for?

All those lovers, drunk out, piled high – and none of them near quenching her. These lovers cast you out at desert noonday, ashamed to name the way by which you're coming. As she treads – empty, worn pot lifted high – she peruses her lovers: wonders what each was a way of looking for.

Well approaching, she begins to lower the pot. Weren't they all a search for home? Weren't they each a restless plunging? Wild darts in the night-time at scoping truth? In case it dwelt within you. For my finest sense discerned that you might be a dwelling place for God, Tabernacle-friend . . .

> . . . holder of the Holy?
> The surprise dwells only in my *being*
>> surprised to find that you have been
>>> the place that I have run to
>>>> in my heart in case you may turn out
>>>>> to harbour what I'm aching-looking for.

> . . . (deep calls to deep in the thunder of your waterfalls) . . .

So I search. Into you. Come lover, to my bedroom door, and enter in. For what calls is insatiable: my body but an instrument that shapes in flesh a song that weaves from what is sourced invisible. But ending where? In what heart? With what body? In which dream? In what union?

So I hunt. More like another, I prowl the streets in search of life, and, when exhausted, roam out to the wastelands. And I *do* devour: with others, as our souls entwine, we know we've each left lovers in the crisis of the midlife hours, because we've still not found what's deepest meaning.

Best, perhaps, I cannot find it: for I'd bind you up and take you hostage, dam your course to source my life.

I confess it, I am thirsty. And I do not mean for water that fills jars.

On earth I am a desert-dwelling creature. My lovers they are in the town, but still I find it's to the well I'm bound at parching noonday.

Discarder, discarded.

Now here's a man. Another man. Beside the well. He comes when I'm most weary.

I silent stay (and turned away, not worth your while, for won't beguile when naked with the questions of the desert.) My displays of worth are for the town. (Here I am merely faint, and unbecoming.) Among my lovers I'm pearled and jewelled, I arch my eyebrows and flirt within the streets. I have learned how to dance within the labyrinth and turn its corners with smoothest poise: not even breaking gaze. I can spin upon a point, though my guts are twisting whirly. I place my pot. (He is watching. I am exhausted, emptied, man: here, I've nothing for you. Meet me night-time.)

Who is this – who calls me over? Visitor of noon-time wells – bodes badly, though life's taught me how to catch your parching. But it's timing: I have nothing for you here, man, meet me in the city, in the nightlife, where I'll know how to translate you on my bed.

You want water? Ha! Unmeaning. You have no way of holding, you: more lost to desert, fool, than I. You ask *me*? You may as well ask the stones, brother, curve your want. But this liquid animator of dust, of Adam-flesh, I'll pull up for you now.

As you receive what I am giving, we splash stones.

You ask about my lovers? Desert-dweller by deep-plunge wells, you know, do you, that they have been, and what they mean, for me? Seer not only of what bodies have *done* but what, more, they have *spoken of* in searching each one out. My well: around its surface my lovers and I are ringing, each dive, each thrust for water pulling only enough to quench the night-time. Morning comes, arrivals are mirage: as tides retreat, we thirst again.

But: you.

You. Whose well do you plumb now as from your lips come questions that I flee from? Arriver on the planes of midday, midlife, midnight, deserts I roam round: yet now to note a welling centre, which is coming.

Coming to the shattered huntress, man who has been dwelling by the well. Are you *really* going to kneel by my bloodied hands which have torn at your world to find my meaning? You should know, strange tender, that the redness in the crevice of my nails is muddied juice strained out by death-grip striving – and the blood of those I've scratched – all grossly mingled. Violation has many forms.

Yet you pat my scars.

You are pouring well water over my hands. You are holding them, in your own clear grasp, and caressing out the bloodiness. This is love-making.

You are what I have hunted.

Now *you* roar: but only at my falling, tripping, stalling. Now *you* cry: but only at my turning, wearying, dying. Now *you* rise and stretch: but so to pour on water as I crawl red dust, its only wetting tears.

You had me haul up first creation, and in it find you mirrored. Liquid animator of dust, of Adam-flesh, first author-frame: I thirst again.

But what this heart is hunting it finds, panting, beneath the pouring-out that's you. For you are sight of second-flesh, and in the meantime, coursing waters, wildfire rescue.

So, in deserts, hunters rest to lap you.

Questions for reflection

1 Are you able to name what you most deeply yearn for? Is God speaking to you about this central need? *security, peace, acceptance,*

2 Which 'loves' are you chasing in your life?

3 What is the culture around you craving for? How do you know? Where are these cravings conveyed? What particular 'wells' are being suggested as the place of satiation? What kind of 'living water' is being promised? Is it really available?

Significance, power. Actions are not for the greater good, but for their own ends. Everyone has their own agenda.

16

[handwritten: Depression + anxiety feeling no one loves me.]

4 Certain Christian spiritual traditions particularly emphasize God as the lover who pursues us: how do you respond to this? *[handwritten: I like it.]*

[handwritten: I think archetypes are valuable]

5 Where is the desert for you? *[handwritten: Not being able to experience God when I go off into too narrow a Christian experience]*

6 Where are the wellsprings in your life? Could you develop any habits to help this well find its way to you more often? *[handwritten: — Solitude]*

7 Where are the 'wells' in the culture around you where you might meet and converse with those who are searching for a satisfying, endlessly available living water? *[handwritten: Probably not churches. Other Christians often make me feel uncomfortable - one too "holy" and are judgemental. Retreats. Writing + Journalling. New Age thought.]*

A prayer for today

Lord, we learn from your appearing that our peace arrives in returning to the home that made us. Help us to come to the well when we are thirsty. Give us the courage to confess, with intimate trust and truthfulness, our desert life to you. Draw us to you, for restoration and renewal.

Give us the wisdom to discern our true desires: and to discern between those that bring us life, in pulling us into you, and those that take our life away by draining our awareness of your presence.

Praise be to you – our great Restorer, and friend of the desert wanderer. Amen.

[handwritten: Power + significance. In the public arena public figures just do each other down and have no respect for each other.]

[handwritten: Gang culture - tribalism - Everyone wants to be "top dog" Knife crime - about power. People feel powerless and insignificant. This is a way of getting the upper hand. "Look at Me"]

*[handwritten: * Political promise./self help gurus/social media memes. All readily available but false.]*

Hijacked

We live in an age that worships tolerance and 'the right to choose'. But isn't there something frustrating, dishonest, about how religious perspectives are censored while the consumerist world cashes in on their festivals?

Perhaps more frustrating still is the false value of 'freedom' that washes through our culture, teaching that religious conviction demands an assault on our rights and choices – which must be avoided – while enslaving us, through a blinding double standard, to consumerist commitments that serve fallen powers.

You see, one way or another, we worship. We commit our intentions and energies to some final cause. It's in our bones so to do: as is confirmed by our inevitable structuring of meaning daily, our flight from the despairing nihilism of *true* atheism which would leave us unable to place one foot in front of the other.

But do we know what we *are* committing to, if there's no standing-place called 'neutral', if we are, in fact, bound to worship by our being? Are we seeing the options clearly, if we avoid 'religious' commitments while allowing the so-called freedoms to name our Cause? Let's take a glance at the landscape . . .

*   *   *

It's Advent. Amid the predictable chaos with which the world hijacks the festival of the Prince of Peace, cinemas across the country have rescinded their agreement to show a short film, within the trailer set, about the meaning and practice of the Lord's Prayer. Apparently, it would offend.

One retailer's TV advert, depicting the nativity, has Jesus replaced by a handbag.

I am unsurprised by the cinemas' anaemic decision: more surprised by the Church's shock at the break in agreement given the palpable reality of the current public censorship of all things Christian (though I'm delightedly amused by the Church's boldness in giving it a go).

But one axis point of the debate especially grates: because it has less to do with the sad wars we wage knowingly, in recognition of the terms, our weapons drawn visibly; and concerns instead that pool of unknowing, of chronic un-self-awareness, which allows a culture to protest absurdities and to ground claims for justice and fairness in the mires of unconscious self-contradiction. Some have noticed, and protested against, it in response to the cinemas' decision: it is the ludicrous non-logic of denying the expression of seasonal Christian tenets while condemning thousands of hostage-held cinema viewers to lambasting by advertising purposed to advance the consumerist religion by manipulating them into buying their 'gifts' for . . . yes, Christmas.

What is most frustrating, surely, is not the cinemas' decision to ban the film, but the manipulation which has so many believing they are choosing and living 'freedom' while being endlessly bombarded with the desire-stimulating pornography of exploitative consumerist advertising. Meanwhile, the culture is content to be taught that the real enemy of freedom is 'religion' – 'religion' which might grant sufficient perspective to have you contesting whether you are free at all (it's always worth noting what the consensus is attempting to write off: here, so often, lies a clue). The totalitarian proclaimers of your freedom, the inciters of your hatreds, will have you mirror images of what you claim to loathe. The Agenda – and the censoring of religious perspectives to seal the blindness – is a most obvious and obfuscated quality of contemporary culture in the North Atlantic West.

All our freedoms are knotted. We are in a mess. We do not see clearly.

This year – the thirty-second of my living – brings the first Advent season in which the public celebration of Christ-mas has effaced its meaning entirely. We have not the reason to match our season's rhymes. Christ is buried beneath glitter, he is nowhere to be seen. The country reverts to a Pagan winter festival of lights. Personified ostriches called Patricia and Penny are the harbingers of Christmas for one city I visit (their coming announced on massive billboards shrouding the central shopping district). Elsewhere we celebrate snowflakes, robins, cars, stars, lipsticks and fairy-tale princesses whose narratives herald 'the greatest love story ever told', and scattered alphabet letters (Christmas tree baubles) emit their random glint amid the paraphernalia of one major department store. At the heart of the cathedral super-mall, the inner-sanctuary grotto is a shrine to postmodernist confusion. And am I imagining it, or is Father Christmas bigger than ever this year? Advent calendars behold him now: red and fat and demanding that you buy, buy, buy your gifts, gifts, gifts, with a Ho! Ho! Ho! this Christmastime. Do please keep on keeping the consumerist whirligig turning. Santa works hard for the advertisers: behold their Lord, and pay your homage.

To cement the layers of cultural amnesia, I am, while silenced to speak whose mass it is, commanded by one shhh-ing mum to keep Santa's name sacred, his identity concealed, his reality the secure delusion of the trusting child. In the past I've played this game happily: but as the hypocrisies of the culture solidify, and I learn more about the ways by which we live and die, and the cost of these strange games we play, I find I'm less the good girl this year than, Santa, your grace-less gospel would have me be. The fires of protest smoulder in the chimney: less hospitable than the flat-screened cavern through which you've poured all year.

In persisting and perverse reversals, I am asked to use the very jewels taught and brought by my faith to repress it now: tolerance to thwart my speech; freedom to stop me speaking the name who offers to *all his children* life and love.

Come now, we don't want Christ at Christ-mass. Come now, let's go, and buy, and buy, and make our offerings to we know not what. We are not religious. It is time to make the sacrifice, the transaction at the altar-counter: to the Till, to stun this fear, to purchase life.

Questions for reflection

1 Where have you recently seen the world 'hijacking' the gospel message?

2 Which paradoxes or absurdities do you recognize in contemporary approaches to 'religion' and 'freedom'?

3 How do you interpret the relationship between our culture's celebration of what are named as Christian festivals and the often secularized versions of these? Are they actually secularized?

4 Do you see opportunities for Christian re-engagement with these public festivals? What could this look like where you are?

5 What particular visions and values do you think your culture offers people – and young people in particular – today? What are they invited to aspire to? Fear? Hope for? Detest? Desire? Avoid?

6 In times of persecution, what might a graceful *and* passionate living of the gospel look like?

A prayer for today

Lord, it's not always easy to own our faith, and to be faithful. We pray for the wisdom of the Spirit, that we might live showing out the fruits of the Spirit – kindness, gentleness, perseverance, patience – especially when we feel least able to be free in our believing and living.

Good Father, we pray for the youngest members of our cultures, those especially porous to the messages of our media and systems of influence and power. Protect them, we pray, to grow in wisdom and grace, as did Jesus as a child. And give us the strength, where necessary, to offer them another and a better way to live. Amen.

Alpha: first love (early fires)
John 1.1–5, 9–11

I wonder if you have a favourite getaway place? Somewhere you go to relax and enjoy a simple pleasure? On study days I retreat to a coffee shop in a local garden centre. As I think and read and my internal world concentrates and stills, the surrounding cafe expands and fills to heaving with parents and children. By midday I'm marooned in a jungle of buggies, cappuccino cups and flying flowerpots. It's a great place to people-watch, from my single still centre.

On one particular morning I notice a little girl standing by the till as her mum pays for breakfast. At the heart of the busy whirl of activity, she is entirely focused on lifting up her teddy bear to sit on the counter. Here I'm sure I see the tenderness of God taking shape in the early expressions of a young life. Life, as this little one grows up, will hold frights and challenges: to safety and love, order and life. I find myself writing a poem about how some of life's earliest shapes, in a kind of circling, are clues to realities that finally call us home.

I wonder if this little one's earliest instincts are a clue to the dwelling-God that made her? Will she remember him? And will God's friends help her to find him: the one who sources her instinct, that internal spark that marks her as created by Love and called to be in relationship with Love – gleaned in something as small as her care for a teddy?

*　*　*

It is Wednesday morning in the coffee shop.

She places teddy – careful and steady – on the bench above. Mummy is paying for breakfast at the till up there, but Bear has got to be a part of it as well. Amid the rush of all surrounding – launching waiters,

22

flying cups and pinging bells – she is slow. Little centre of silence. Little storm-eye.

Bear is raised with mirrored arms, perfectly paralleled – and is watched as he rises, half lifted by steady contemplation. This little one is all concentration. Bear must have his part.

And Bear's part arrives so tenderly. He has caramel fur and a red white-spotted coat. As he gains finally to bench height, she rests him back so carefully, so carefully, and lets go of his arms but barely now, to check that he will stay. He will: and she steps back to look at him, her body full concentration, adoration, to see that Bear has made it. He is part of it all. Bear had to have his part.

Tenderness. This little flicker-feeling. This gently attending loving raise arising, emerging just there – unbespoken, natural token – gifted form, in lovingness unlearnt.

She is like You:
she is showing,
pressing out –
– in early instinct
making love.

Yet, unbeknowing,
death, she's towing too:
dark is churning,
monsters lurking,
tides and walls against which Life takes flight.

Dissonance there already,
you see:
full recipe to churn from nature's depths life's endless strife.

To save myself.

Except.

The hints are in the early fires,
the little burnings 'life' conspires
(or so we say, full thinking we know 'life'
though all we mean is timing's plotting thread)
to shadow with the ending: 'dead',

and so, in sick-tuned prophet-protest
steadily expires.

Yet.

The hints are in the early fires:
the revelries that fear devours,
the play, and making, grit, risk-taking,
with vital framing:
knowing it shall ever be.

The glints are in the early fires:
  – though *now* –
      what lit the dawn burns red in End-sky's pulsing promises.

For we are circling, Spirit-led:
what birthed us calls us back to home,
though not returning how we came
but rather, through a Named-one grown,
whose is the End –

through Christ.

Christ: Love's matter making,
while his breath breathes out what's Love's returning;
just so, transfiguring how we see
all life's caught-yearnings:
protests at end-curved turnings
now revealed as earth-sky's lurching out 'Protest: divinity!'

We can miss it, but our lives, in living, certain beginnings testify.
We can miss it, but the story's written backwards, arrives to
weave with what will turn to rise.

Here's Grace: what's best in blessed beginnings is preserved,
who authored shape and form now casting Gold to spin revivals.

The earth will birth again
with End-time seed.
For that which breathed, and breathes, us, sings the future.

Come: know the tune,
for it is Named and there's a caller.

Come to Life.

Questions for reflection

1 What struck you about this reflection?

2 Where do you see the 'early fires' in your life, and in the life of the world? What do they illuminate?

3 Where do you see God's presence in the world in virtue of its createdness? What are the marks of his authorship and faithful presence?

4 Where do you recognize in life's most basic instincts signs of our createdness? What defines or characterizes these signs? To what do they point or gesture?

5 Are there things about life – particular 'givens' – that appear inherently in need of redemption? Do you recognize such things in your own life? How do you bring them to the care and wisdom of God?

A prayer for today

Lord, we see the scope of our lives as the revelation of your gospel presents it: we are made by love and are called to return, through Christ, to the perfection of that love, which is creation's destiny. Help us to see you in the 'early fires' which testify to your presence and goodness, and give us courage and vision to traverse the days of brokenness as we find our way back, through you, to you. Amen.

Spinning

Have you ever paid attention to the advertisements whirling around you daily? Rather than block them out, attended to what someone is trying so hard to sell you?

Within a culture that dances on the brink of nihilism, that would tell us God is dead, a power tries continually to stimulate our desires, captivate our attention and enslave our energies. And, indeed, the selling, if we take a look at it, is trying to lure us into all kinds of contradictions and absurdities. Can you sense the contradictions? And can these secular sources really sell what they are offering? Are the promises they make actually within their power to give?

* * *

I'm waking to the radio, and, wrenching into consciousness, am already imbibing the offer that arrives as threat: 'Buy this now (and if you don't . . .)' – the logic to shape the day. But fear is whet.

The TV's on and promises are weaving around the airways of the house. This internet provider will bring you infinity; this telephone company will endow you all-powerful; that mobile provider ensures blessed futurity. Are you beginning to take note and rise to me?

But remember, God is dead.

I'm out the door and billboards loom with high-majestic might, set right for sight-consuming. Our holiday company will let you belong anywhere; this banking group rewards you simply for being you. As I survey the Pagan highway, gut-low longing for relief of resting rises with a tingle.

But remember, God is dead.

I'm on the bus, and settling down, but sight's again arrested. The daily paper churns its words so grossly as to stun faint finitude, yet ringing out is conflicting wisdom: 'Is the secret to doing more actually to do less?' We'll offer a sweet antidote to the poison we're gently venting. We will massage you.

But remember, God is dead.

Above our heads, where heaven's pending beauty was once imaged out, we're given new ethereal prospects, heaven-types to contemplate. Immortality is bottled cream, and holiness is skin touched up to glowing. Abandon faith's false promises, here is Truth for trusting and for knowing. Here's life eternal and golden blessedness as foretaste. Here is your perfection, and your sanctification as plastics embalm you. Here is eternity, as temporality and decay are fixed beneath a crystal glaze. Possess this, and you'll en-trance whatever's arriving.

But remember, God is dead.

'Will living closer bring us closer?', the Tube side's arterial tattoo asks out as carriage by carriage is pulsed to deep-vein clotting: 'DELAYS', 'DELAYS'. As we wait in the crackling darkness walls stare back with sick-tuned invitations: 'Life is short: take an art class.' Such power – so wielded – twisted magic, exacting absolute power to sell by crippling me to death with one brute fell. You would-be parasite, using up my fear to take my life, reversing forces. Waking cold, I begin to object.

But remember, God is dead.

Pacing the pavement, with compulsive returns to checking time, I notice the road holds intermittent message boards, placed to face car drivers. 'Drive safely: someone loves you', one reads. 'Let's all get home safely', another. For what? To buy? To own? To produce? To die? I can't remember why.

Remember, God is dead.

So here is your best Creed for me:
that I'm to buy Infinity,
and masturbate eternally,
while giving you the best of me.

You wish.

But I see, on all your surfaces, dear Culture, the scars that mar that death-battling face: you prodigal child, to be loved up out of screaming confusion and into life again. What tells the lie is the trembling that *outs* from the conflict *in* you: as you renounce your lover, while craving to dance, and asking whoever is not him. You shun the commitment. But it leaves you courting contradiction, and weeping in the hidden hours of night. You abandon your people to ungrounded lives suspended amid endless pictures spinning. But your adverts – in their straining long – sing only and over the gospel's own song as your lyrics steal her own protests, mimic her promises.

The secret to your endless failure is this: the gift you promise is not yours to give, neither yours to urge payment for. You only shape people who have eyes, but are not seeing; who have ears, but are not hearing; who have minds, but are never comprehending.

Because the love you know to stimulate, you could never, in all time, satiate.

Questions for reflection

1 Where do you recognize advertisements in our culture offering what is God's to give? Which divine attribute, or aspect of belonging to God, are adverts endeavouring to sell? What have you noticed recently?

2 How do you understand the role of the prophet in diagnosing the relationship between Christ and culture?

3 In what ways do advertisements stimulate our desires? How might this affect our relationship with God?

4 What do you think sources the particular agendas and perspectives endorsed and encouraged by the advertising industry?

5 What are the 'idols' that our culture would have us chasing after? Where do they manifest?

How might such 'idols' be 'crushed'?
Which other loves might thereby lose their power to tempt us?
What might a culture freed to manifest the creative and redeeming hand of God look like? What would we find ourselves free to imagine in the place of our societal idols?

6 Where do you glimpse opportunities to make these challenges to the culture?

A prayer for today

Lord, our society, in its (often unconscious) flight from death, is restless and yearning. As people living in this culture we find ourselves assaulted daily with offers, threats and promises. Help us so to live for you – to build our house on the cornerstone of your Word, and to invest in the treasures of your enduring kingdom – that we can discern our best relation to our immediate world, and know where to mark the signposts. Amen.

Cabbages and castles
Matthew 19.13–15

I often take the 6.40 a.m. train to London Victoria on my commute into central London for work. One dark, midwinter morning, our usual communal sleeping slump is disturbed by the agitations of a little bird determined to create and tell a story.

When the Holy Spirit arrives in our midst, it may be, as it first was, with a burst of creativity and a stirring, wild hilarity. Are we surrounded by little Pentecosts?

* * *

She shrills the train, grating more than shrieking steel-struck train tracks.

'Daddy! Can I tell you a story?'

Daddy is asleep. Or practised at feigning.

'Dad*deee*! I have a story! Can I tell you my story?'

They say the creative artist must receive the inspiration that can arrive at any time. But this time is 6.40 a.m. on the early commuter train to London city centre on a deep-winter morning. Crisp-clothed office-bound bodies lie slumped and retarded, less like the promise of bodies to rise, more like the exhausted remainder of yesterday's thrown-off skin.

As the train enjoys its sepulchral silence, the irritant pursues her goal.

'Daddy, I'm going to tell you a story.'

'Sweetheart, it's time to rest now. Get under the blanket.'

Daddy has brought a nest for their two-seat corner. But his little bird is determined to take flight instead. And to chirrup with spectacular indifference for slumbering friends. Perhaps she anticipates their delight.

'Once upon a time . . .' (*slowly announcing, upturned eyes wondering*).

'Sweetheart, I don't think . . .'

'There was a house' (*confident, decided now*).

'Sweetheart, seriously, it's time to settle down.'

'Something was really special about the house . . .' (*a new trajectory!*).

'Everyone's trying to sleep. Stop being so loud.'

'The house was really . . .' (*the story is clearly being composed*) '. . . really small—' (*giggle*).

'Settle down now. Do you really think everyone wants to hear your story when they're trying to sleep?'

'In fact, it was *so* small . . .' (*a pause: now what might happen next?*).

'That's enough now—' (*firmer*).

'That you couldn't fit anything in it. Not even . . . *a cabbage!*'

Then shrieks of laughter, bold and abandoned: delighted by the random surprise of her own ingenious creation. 'Not even a cabbage!' A second-wave of relishing screams.

Then louder still, and sitting up further in her blanket-nest: 'Can I tell you another one? I've got more!' Confident in her storehouse, she needs only surrounding ears to hear to bid the new creations form and rise.

She'll learn how to be tamed. But the queen that grows will store in buried troves this questing, light-ordering princess. I am certain that, were we only to stop dulling her, the compositions of new creation would keep on coming, tumbling out and down the carriages: this little one painting all her castles more solid than sky as, before us, she steps into a kingdom.

Questions for reflection

The Holy Spirit brings the conditions of God's promised future into the present: consequently, the power and presence of this unpredictable Spirit – which moves as and where he will – often arrives as disturbance or agitation, breaking up settled norms and starting up a new and startling song.

1 Where in the reflection above do you see signs of this arrival? Where in your own life have you seen such eruptions recently?

2 How do you understand the relationship between creativity and the nature and character of God?

3 Consider a community or social circle close to you: perhaps a church, a friendship group, a workplace or your family. Can you identify any habits that are deadening to creativity, to spontaneity or expression? What might it mean to reshape this culture and unlock these spaces?

4 The Apostle Matthew records that Jesus 'called a child, whom he put among them, and said, "Truly I tell you, unless you change and become like children, you will never enter the kingdom of heaven. Whoever becomes humble like this child is the greatest in the kingdom of heaven"' (Matthew 18.2–4).

What do you think Jesus meant? What can we learn from children about what it is to come into God's kingdom?

What about a child – and about childlikeness – might especially assist the Holy Spirit in his work in our world?

How could you become more childlike? What life would this bring?

How does your culture interpret childlikeness? What life does this bring, or inhibit?

5 Jesus goes on to say: 'Whoever welcomes one such child in my name welcomes me' (Matthew 18.5). How might we better shape

our churches and communities to receive what children have to bring?

A prayer for today

Lord, help us to see your coming. Awaken our hearts, minds, bodies and souls in the midst of routine so that we are ready to greet you – and the party that you bring. Amen.

Confession: love is (not) blind

In our consumerist, capitalist culture we are conditioned to believe that we create our worth through our productivity, efficiency and accruing of material wealth. To achieve these things requires success.

But the journey into relationship with God brings us into stark awareness of our shortcomings and failures. Moreover, our awareness of this poverty – strange logic! – turns out to be the beginning of our new freedom, as we stop trying to save ourselves (create and sustain our own identities) and surrender to finding our worth in the one who sources it, unconditionally.

What does the word 'sin' mean to you? Here is a word so bandied, so maligned, so freighted – so used to bash hearts when its discovery should be the beginning of release – as to have lost meaning, and certainly appeal, for many contemporary ears. Nothing about its announcement tastes like the chance of renewal and refreshment. But have you ever noticed that growing into relationship with God brings our lack of him – and its sign, our longing – into central frame? Have *you* found a love that makes even the inevitability of your failure an occasion for rejoicing, because it points beyond itself to a life that leaves failure by the wayside?

*   *   *

'Sin.' What a powerful little word. A highly charged concept sitting right at the heart of our world view. Among the many untruths that circulate about our faith is the idea that a Christian sins less than their neighbour, is less tempted than their friend. And perhaps there is – by grace, through discipline, and with a rarely celebrated sheer push of will found in Christ's own eleventh-hour obedience to his Father – an improvement. Perhaps, when our understanding of God's nature and our own is clarified through prayer, when we receive the supernatural support of grace, we can live lives more in line with the laws and loves of God's heart.

And yet falling in love with God does strange things to your vision. They say that love is blind: unless you fall in love with God, one ought to note. Because never was I more aware of sin, my own, the world's own, your own, dear friend; never more overwhelmed by its pervasiveness, never less confident of a soul's unaided ability to disentangle herself from the sticky matrix. The equation is simple: the light of God's presence illuminates our sin, shows up the difference.

Before I was a Christian – actually, even while a Christian, but before one of those recurring waves of ever-deepening conversion – I would have offered you a definition of sin in abstract: 'Not so much discrete acts,' I would have said, though I think with a healthy concern to avoid our narrow-eyed obsession with certain areas, 'Not so much discrete acts, as the general condition of living at a distance from God.' Sin at a distance; sin as a structure; sin outside myself; sin *in absentia*.

But loving God, it turns out, does not turn you blind. It opens your eyes. This love does not settle you down, or suggest a nest, or sing songs of your glorious perfections. You are precisely too valuable for these epithets. Too beloved to be left with your mirrors for windows. And too much purposed, too much called, too much planned for, too much dreamt-of, too much gifted, too much invested with God's own image and yearning, too much meditated on in the delighted mind and imagination of God, to be left to think that you are most yourself alone.

Because – violent to contemporary sensibilities – this falling in love is not about you. You are called to love a broken world. A world hurting in very specific ways. The cross is pain in desperate specificity: crucifixion is bloody nakedness, suffocation, nails, thorns, a curse and the burning stinking rubbish dumps outside a heaving city oblivious to your dying here. It is occupying forces, smashed knees, broken legs, a knife through your ribcage and your lovers watching on. Concrete, particular, death in time; for sins concrete, particular and deathly in time.

The more I love God, the more I see for what he died. All those innumerable little daily ways I deny your reality, as I endeavour to possess you, subsume you, exploit you, use you. All those subtle little corrosions of our humanity in which I participate by will and in blissful unconscious negligence.

> And forgive me, brother, sister, for I see this now. And I am so sorry.
> Forgive us our trespasses, as we forgive those who trespass against us.
> Love of God does not make you blind.
> Forget that. Forget the caveat.
> Love does not make you blind.
> Love is not blind.

Questions for reflection

1 How do you understand 'sin'?

2 Where do you see 'individual' sin?

3 Where do you see systemic sin (the sins enshrined and enabled by systems and networks: perhaps in institutions)? Where do you see sin residing and flourishing within whole cultures? Within *your* culture?

4 Have you ever found yourself becoming more aware of your distance from true living? What caused the raised awareness?

5 'Repentance', to turn from sin, comes from the word 'metanoia', which means to change one's mind, to turn around and change direction. Where do you see your culture most in need of 'turning around' and 'changing direction'? Can you spot any opportunities to begin this conversation?

A prayer for today

Merciful Lord, help us to see ourselves. Reveal to us what 'sin' really means – leave us not with caricatures or stereotypes or shrunkendown definitions that work against, rather than towards, our turning to find ourselves in you.

Merciful Lord, help us to see others. Break the spells that leave us burdened with fantasies and wrong assumptions about the people we think we know and the relationships that we are woven into. Give us a fitting agnosticism about our rightness with regard to all things. We dare to pray: teach us what your crucifixion means. Amen.

Gardening
John 20.1–18

———◆◆◆———

There is a garden near the building where I work. Set apart by neat black railings, its sanctuary rests uncontested, rarely entered, in the middle of the city: so still, in fact, that I had not noticed it despite walking past it for a year. I am not a gardener, but as I get older I begin to share with gardeners that sense of call to this particular place, for it feels like the garden speaks of more than itself, holds the key to engaging with rhythms of life. Have you been in a garden recently? What do you find there? What does it say to you? What is God gardening in you?

*   *   *

Stillness.
And a resting that sits just beside the busy highways.
And this sense that it's all there, after all: just waiting to pour to the surface . . .

I have walked past this garden twice a week, easily summing a hundred days, and I never noticed it, in the beginning. I have no relationship with gardens, you see, no love affair to grasp my attention with promises of pleasure to be found in little soil beds. I do not hear their call. Perhaps you do?

But as I pace by this spot daily, all obedience to my schedule, I begin to feel magnetized by a realm outside my self: called outwards by the summoning garden, to the side; called to spill beyond myself into this space. For protected within these railings is an emptiness that has escaped the clutter, where huge blossoms blow out their extravagant pinks: calling life with perfumes that somersault through air. Here are scents and blends and breezes that nothing shop-bought can pretend to. The busy bees are signs of continuing abundance.

As I pause for the first time to lean in at the edge of a space that suggests I am missing the heart of something, it is springtime: and white petals fall from blossom-full trees as nature's confetti over the waiting ground of the secret garden. I want to be a bride in *this* garden! This garden, where the birds rest and sing, and the roses burst unashamed, where there is holding and peace, and the whole, ringed, great ground rests caring and storing beneath your feet, promising that life will come again: pressing upwards surprising your naked soles. I want to be a bride in this garden.

Gardens are honest places, holding both death and life out on display. Mary Magdalene lingers and seeks and strains to find the one called Life by the tomb-side, in the place where leaves fall goldly to the ground, their brittle skeletons suspending frozen lifelines. But as she gazes, eyes locked down to the death-bearing void, the voice of one comes from behind her, from the other side of greens and reds and purples and all kinds of brights striking bold silk and velvet layers. The gardener himself is come to tell that in the garden he's been raised. And so, from that first day, he lends to every garden since – to yours and mine – the power to tell truly of life that is coming from earth. He makes the garden speak, its garden-grammar meaning: what dies, rises.

I want a key to *this* garden! But we don't need a key, for in this garden we already pass our day. The gardener is always walking here, presiding over every phase and season. Planting. Tending. Resting. Lifting.

This garden: where, at close of day, as thinning petals paled to milk dissolve beneath my fingertips, the very gardener is heard to say, 'Just wait until the morning.'

Questions for reflection

1 What happens in the garden described above? What patterns of dying and living are found there?

2 Do you know a place of nourishment and growth, which offers the hopefulness of a garden? Where are the 'gardens' in your life and the life of your community?   — Our back garden
at work

St Dunstan's, Hyde
Hull skye garden.
Secret gardens.   East Ruston

3 Where do you see the promise of resurrection in your own life?

4 Where do you see God as Gardener?

5 Are there places speaking of gospel-shaped life-rhythms in your culture? Where are they? What do people discover in and through them? Do you need to create some?

6 Where does the culture around you need a gardener: one who plants, cares, prunes, redirects, nourishes? Could this be a calling to you? *Church Planting*
Something for single. 50 somethings – not
Kid. related. – Yes it could be!

A prayer for today

Creator God, you place us within a world that you have made and tended by your own wounds. Help us, by your Spirit, to discover our ground and flourishing in the life of the Son, the tomb-side gardener. Help us to see the places you would have us tend in turn. Amen.

The game with no name
John 14.15–17

Do you ever find it hard to talk about your faith? And not because a particular reality, or idea, is difficult to grasp or describe, but because it seemed as if the very language required were unavailable, had disappeared?

*   *   *

I'm folding my laundry while listening to the radio. A scientific programme reviews current theories on quantum mechanics, and the interviewee explains that, on one spooky account, it is the act of my looking and seeing that summons the universe to presence and order. 'In some sense,' she concludes, 'if I'm not looking at the moon, it isn't there.'

I'm reminded of Bishop Berkeley's question: if a tree falls unobserved in a forest, has it really fallen at all?

Merely two days later, a London-based university lecturer delivering his research on 'What makes us happy?' announces that 'You are what you attend to.'

'Desiring to see God?' asks the Psalmist. 'O *taste and see* that the Lord is good.'

There appears to be a relationship between *how* you look and what you are *able* to see; between *how* you look and what it *becomes possible* to see. Not because there is a trick going on, but because it is in the nature of the thing to reveal itself in just that way. If you want to know God, do not speculate on your own impoverished grounds. Rather, take the thing on its own terms. Pray, read Scripture, be baptized, take bread and wine: grow up in the life of the Church.

Mystics, contemplatives, religious artists know that to see something may require a disposition of immersion, a suspension of the naivety of dis-belief: not *so* different from the adjustment of the microscope lens required to render, for vision, the properties of the slide. Perhaps the nature of the object determines the justness of the gaze. Our habit is to go the other way round: to make our way of seeing the grounds for proof.

A great poverty of our time is the intellectual-imaginative poverty of having lost ways of looking. The contemporary mind is offered a mean world of bounded solid objects: only the material is really real. And appearances are everything: postmodernity is surface living; life without depth that slides and writhes, unable to speak of richer truths, or even to pose the questions that trace their way. Ironically, this creed requires a tremendous act of faith: no one has shown that these are the only ways of Being. But it's easy to lose sight of what we've forgotten it's possible to look for.

Science, of course, believes nothing so unimaginative, so reductive. You have only to consider the sky blending space-wards. But the subtleties of the whys and wherefores of appearing or disappearing moons struggle to lodge in the stripped-out consciousness, or to register within the blunted expressions of mind-starving media.

The consequence is a vanishing act. The moon, unobserved, fails to be. Not really: but in its being *for me*. I become blind to wonderful possibilities. I cannot see God because I have started with the wrong way of looking.

The philosopher and painter of human nature Iris Murdoch was superbly attuned to the urgency of this. Leave something crucial out of your picture of, say, the human being, and you will not be able to get it in later. A reduced picture is a reduced picture for ever. Reduce a man to his behaviours and you will never recover his 'internal' invisible consciousness, nor the substantial reality of his contemplative acts. Reduce a woman to her behaviour, and whatever about her does not issue in external events does not (appear to) exist. But then gone is everything interesting. Gone are the things that feel for most of us really real. Gone are the things of identity. Gone are feelings, hopes, desires, dreams, prayers, visions, the changings of our mind.[8]

What is done to a woman or man can be done to whole dimensions of culture. We see this – warned Murdoch – where, in our time, certain problems become unstatable. We have lost the language to speak of sin, of death, of prayer, of salvation, of redemption, of confession, of transgression, of reverence, of holiness: and out with them go joy and peace and forgiveness and hope and restoration and celebration.

Let's be logical, we faithful protestors, and drive the thing home: we live in binaries – without one half, where is meaning and purpose at all? The atheist keeping Goodness resorts to faith at this point. Let's at least be consistent and be nihilists. Perhaps then, for the first time, sitting in our life-stripping acid bath, we'll be able to *see* what is at stake. To know the claims we make.

There is a disappearing act. The act in itself is invisible, and its trace is the power of what we cannot say. Its observable concomitants are negative impressions: they arrive in censorship.

Do not preach the gospel.

But we are left to live life with absurdities: pronouncing faith in Nothing while we scurry to erect altars from the rubble of blasted truths. Contemporary therapies tread this awkward ground. I am asked to imagine a 'compassionate other' coming alongside me in adversity (wasn't that God?). I am asked to take time for meditation (isn't that prayer?). I am encouraged to embrace compassionate loving kindness (isn't that God's nature?). I am advised to pursue detachment in my thinking (isn't that contemplation?). I am told to practise these devises (wasn't that spiritual discipline?). I am asked to believe that everyone deserves compassion, love, peace and forgiveness (without an overarching order underpinning this assumption, *why should I?*). This is but a performance of absurdity with the grounding unstuck. This is the pursuit of the therapeutic consequence without the founding commitment.

Meanwhile, we are asked, by a nameless pressure, to announce this position 'sound' and our own as lacking internal logical cohesion.

Of course, these are but games. There is a moon, and there are stars. Science recalls our faith. We may say that black is blue: the saying does not make it so. We may say we cannot see the stars: sight's faulty tuning does not source the light.

Beware the force of absences: the power of emptiness, negations and omissions. Beware the black holes that enter silently, with timid protestations of fairness, inoffensiveness and (cheap) grace. The un-naming of things is troubling. More troubling is the namelessness of that game of unnaming itself.

Questions for reflection

1 What is your response to this reflection? What struck you about it?

2 Have you found yourself constrained from preaching the gospel? Where can you see little, or great, daily strainings against its proclamation? *Yes – more so as time has gone on less fashionable to believe in Christianity or be Spiritual now – likely to be ridiculed.*

3 What do you understand, from this reflection, to be the power of negation, omission, silencing? What do you think sources this silencing? *Political correctness - not wanting to "offend" people, we have to temper our language.*

4 Are there aspects of the gospel, or aspects of faith, that you find difficult to bring to articulation in our culture? That is, dimensions, ideas, that seem 'unstatable'? Why do you think this is? Is there required language, or are there required concepts that are missing? *Sin, redemption, what happens when we die*

5 How might a follower of Jesus recover, or discover, required ways of speaking and showing the gospel in our times? What particular challenges will need taking into account to achieve this?

A prayer for today

Lord, help us to preach the gospel, so that people may come to know the life and freedom that is available to them, through you. Give us wisdom to know how to respond to what would silence us; and perception to be able to identify the source of this silencing, for the sake of prophecy. Come and speak to us, by your Spirit, about the things of you that we might miss, that might fall as absences. Pour into what is void, Lord, your life, your revelation, your light. Amen.

Mind the gap
The Song of Songs

I am often on the London Tube as part of my daily work commute: but this wasn't always the case. In the early days of my travel on the Underground the newness allowed all the perception-clarity of encountering an unknown culture. I noticed all the unwritten but (more or less) universally observed rules: we do not talk; we do not make eye-contact; and partly to survive the paradox of our scandalously breath-sharing closeness.

But one day, a troupe of musicians arrived into our carriage, outraging the settled ways of being ...

* * *

Just recently, I was taking the London Underground.

I struggle to judge the world: because I am too immediately aware of its beauty and graced-ness. But on this occasion it struck me how what we so often take to be the habitual, value-neutral 'ways of doing things around here' are actually loaded with meaning. And meaning-loaded in such ways as to reveal that there is no value-neutral no man's land to coast along, but a rather sharply delineated 'choice': to live in ways that give life, or to live in ways that drain life.

To breathe at all is to negotiate this choice: indeed, to breathe at all is to decide one way or another.

Standing rammed in a crowded Underground carriage, deep in the winding bowels of London, I began to observe how we occupy these spaces: how we treat one another. The prime objective, after pressing through the crushing swell of other objects (people), is (having despaired of a seat) to isolate entirely. I have found my face so bewitchingly close to an unknown other's that in any other context we'd have been bound to kiss. The magnetism of unexpected proximity has its own startling charge. But as our bodies press closer, our hearts, our guts, as if set to relations of inverse proportion, rush back, away, out. My eyes – I understand, I have been taught by this ritual – must rest anywhere except on yours. Advertisers have made full gain of this, plastering the roof with oblong tablets, fresh idols for my flighting sight to alight on. In the office, my home, at nursery, I will talk with you. But here, bound by another – and objective – law, we must be strangers.

In an unthinking moment our eyes catch. Your glance darts away, with the sprightliness of that hill-bounding gazelle, but reversing love. There is a fluster: we are both awkward now, partly embarrassed, partly awakened to the tension of inconsistent living. Both recollections bring heat to our faces as we realize the strange dance we have joined in.

I struggle to judge the world: because I am too immediately aware of its beauty and graced-ness. And you, stranger, are beautiful: a universe captured for vision in a few cubic metres of condensed solidity. A mystery made manifest, an incarnation of the invisibility that sources and sustains you. So I do not judge *you* (another has taught me my incapacity for that). But when I think of what you are, my heart smarts against this weary liturgy of how-we-treat-each-other:

> When anima burst through matter, that you *might* matter, how come now to let steel and plastic define our course?

> We are in a metal tube. Therefore we are not human. Who has written this Scripture? This Scripture so many obey who would reject liturgies elsewhere?

The tube slows and stops at a central London station and silence is broken as voices rise. These voices are of another timbre: they do not come from here. Into our tube of steel erupts a group of musicians, guitar, accordion and violin in hand. They shout with the chords of festival. Their bouncing sound casts ribbons of colour through the carriage while their words are full of gently mocking contest. 'Look at us, make eye contact, if you dare! In fact, why not look at one another?

Grab a partner and have a dance! It can be anyone, doesn't have to be someone you know!' Their disturbing revelries continue, 'If you're socially challenged and we're embarrassing you terribly, just ignore us!' They are joy personified. They are freedom come acoustic. They call it like it is. Our collective hostage to reserve is almost unbound. In the carriage there is longing to laugh; I sense the pulsating pregnancy as staring eyes sparkle and bodies almost turn, but there is insufficient daring to bring the dance to birth.

These revelling angels are almost rude and I am reminded of Christ's uncompromising assault on all that steals the light, the truth that is two-edged sword piercing the concealing folds of custom and practice and dividing life from death. The author of life protests every pretence that shrouds the kingdom's glory. And it strikes me then, that here, in the bowels of our great city, is the kingdom coming: three wise men, with their musical gifts, breaking through the satanic spirit which makes us insist we have nothing to do with one another. Here they come, calling our hearts to recognize the human being next to me, then to embrace our graceless guts and dance. Our discomfort, our shifting feet and avoiding eyes (how long until the next stop, until the boisterous intruders leave?), only makes their call to kingdom-living more startling: and our own anaesthesia plain.

The train slows, newly aroused bodies lean into the curve, the carriage stops and the doors open. Our fitful visitors leave to take their message elsewhere. As the train moves on, for the accidental witnesses, the seers of just-passed epiphanies, two realities now lay upon each other, coexist: this immediate environment of metal and removal, and lingering sparks and smiles that begin to testify.

The question to me is clear. We do not live in a vacuum, a value-neutral space, a gap. Do I return to anaesthesia? Or am I now an evangelist?

Questions for reflection

1 What is your response to this reflection? What does it make you think and/or feel? What does it make you wonder?

2 Where do you see the kingdom of God arriving in this encounter? What are its signs?

3 Where have you recently seen the kingdom of God arriving? What were the signs?

4 When the kingdom of God arrives, what does it amplify and bless? What does it transform? What does it protest?

5 Have you had an experience that you would call a 'divine interruption'?

6 To what do you feel called to testify: for what are you an evangelist?

A prayer for today

King of heaven, King of a kingdom: come and arrive in our midst. Come, Holy Spirit, and bring the life of Emmanuel: of God with us. Help us to see the signs of you that arrive in our daily round of living, crowning all the life you breathe and bless. Come, Holy Spirit, and bring the kingdom. Come, pouring upon us now, heaven through earth. Amen.

Cry

Matthew 5.3–8
Matthew 25.31–46

I am a hypocrite. I'm coming out of the railway station one night after a long day at work, and although a Christian, and a priest at that, I'm hoping to get home undisturbed by the pain that I know courses these streets and laps this station's gate like an earth-cry wave.

And then she arrives – this one who manages to crack through my shutdown self-preservation – coming to me like (*as?*) the very one whose way I need recalling to.

How he finds me . . .

* * *

I'm leaving the station so late at night,
my heart full with asking to get, through the light
to the car: unencumbered, and tight-slumbered down,
is my plan for the end of this day.

Ear-phones in.
Course the strip lights.

'Hello, Vicar.'
I am chosen: and protest the moment
as step follows step and the magnet pulls loading
downhill.

But there's Iron that anchors this life: me love-loading.
And so with cry opening –
    as eyes quick to lightning,
    or breath roused to rose-scent –
        I turn.

She's approaching.

Cry

Stepped out from the edges,
into scene from off-canvas,
keen with her story,
already before me,
'homeless' and 'broken' and 'stolen' and 'lonely'
and 'hostels' and 'bedsits' and 'broke', 'dole' (stoned lowly):
my heart beats retreat –
I'm dead-set to flee, toes aft-curving,
from these hungry eyes: so encroaching.

Could I spin you back to darkness.

My sin rises thickly:
the abstract swells wholly
to fill up my feeling,
intention, desire, will
all sure bent, with one thought:
to Abandon.

You are not my sister,
I know not your maker,
I cancel you, stranger,
I am no partaker,
your coming is danger,
your life-call de-ranger
of my safe-bound life:
spelling COST. Spelling REAL. Spelling NOW.

So I curse you.
I, Eve's bland sister,
friend with the fallen,
curved-in, quick-walling.
Retreating.

Except.

Something leans.
Some anchor pulls the frame.
I ask your name.
'Priest, I'm Hannah.'

Testament child.
Stranger named for grace,

for God's gift to the world,
lurks in shadows.

Named: I see your eyes are shining,
still clear light beguiling the roll of your drug-laden tongue,
like a summons, reminding.

You are living.

Here's the spinning:

I am *not*.

For you are bending to me,
leaning in for hugs
from fractured edges
which are my own framing
where I've walled you in for taming. Life-learned training.

Salvation would be failing.

I am your prison.
I am brick wall, dead, depending,
turning from your bed, pretending
not to hear you crying in the night.
Shadow-lurker, midnight haunter of station's Ending,
space-time bending at the belching thresholds of the night
with question marks suspending:

Will you hear my cry?

Miracle. You're merciful – seem only grateful for the talking,
as we side by side start walking
warmer than years-old companions
equals in the night, in desert plight, your piercings sparkling.

Hannah, shining.

He said that we would find him here.
He said that he would come as you.
He said that you would be his place:
you, princess-keeper of his Grace.

And as I lean to shake your hand,
your tumbling-rough embrace

comes landing
falling on me
shaming-off my stiffness
planting kisses.

We part. But, somehow, not in heart.
My sister, strange bewilderer of settlers,
roaming through the streets,
you bright the night
because your wounds pronounce his plight
and call us to attendance.

Beloved lover of his banquet,
Queen-in-transit,
comes to offer me a place around his plate:
calling brick to breath to life,
awakening Grace,
and circumcising hearts.

Questions for reflection

The Holy Spirit disturbs us out of comfort, to see things differently:
to see as Christ sees, as he would have us see. The Spirit of God presses
us into the discomfort of true encounter. And so often, as we put ourselves in the place of serving the broken of this world, we discover
that we've done nothing less than put ourselves in the place of Life:
because we have entered the flow of the river of life. In our serving,
we discover our own healing.

1 Have you recently been disturbed out of a position, an attitude, an
  assumption? What caused the disruption?

2 How has being in Christ changed what, and how, you see and
  behave?

3 The kingdom of God belongs to the broken-hearted (God rushes
  in to help those who need a doctor) and its heralds and possessors
  are those this world would often look past (see Matthew 5.1–12).
  This kingdom is real: *so* real that it is a guaranteed arriving blessing
  to those who find themselves poor, lonely, mourning, excluded,
  imprisoned, oppressed and violated.

  Where in the world around you can you identify heralds and possessors of this kingdom?

4 Where have you tried to spin someone 'out of Life', and away from you? Why was this?

5 Jesus is clear: where we are loving the lost and the least, we are loving him. Who do you know that is needing you to believe this – and to act on this faith – right now?

A prayer for today

Lord, your world is hurting: and our social and political structures, and personal habits, so often compound the breaking. Give us eyes to see beyond the frames of our making. Give us eyes to course the edges: and beyond the pale. We consent – though we ask for the strengthening of your Spirit – to your disrupting of our comforting routines where these are making us blind to your calling. May the peace of Christ disturb us. Amen.

Matchsticks

How do we meet the people God is calling us to serve with his love?

Two years ago my parishes began an outreach to our community. We wondered how we could meet and love the people who live in our area. Where do they gather? The railway station. When is it most bitter to travel? Right before Christmas. What do they need? Comfort on a freezing morning as they commute to work. Breakfast? Fresh coffee? Warming tea? So we bought urns and tables and porridge and set up our gifts right down there, beside the trains, from 5.30 a.m. to 8.30 a.m. in the week before Christmas.

Some walked briskly by, needing the quiet of the morning. Many came and drank and gathered and talked and rejoiced and shared in the love that comes when we open ourselves to others. The train drivers – whom we met with drinks at their windows – tooted on arrival, waved down the platform, and spread the word of our presence so that our love became anticipated: 'Yes! We've heard about you!' Radio stations reported the texts and tweets our recipients sent in from the carriages as they continued their journeys onward: celebrating this surge of community, kindness and grace.

A few weeks later, as I stand on the unlit platform, a commuter now again myself, the burst of light, of being open to one another, is made even more poignant by the reigning of collapsed-down 'normal'. But I've learned something: it only takes a spark to break the night.

* * *

A spark will quench an ocean of darkness.

Tiny things can be game-changers: vast systems, complex networks, whole environments, may anchor in one assumption. The basic belief that my life has nothing to do with yours, nearing stranger, that tiny tepid 'known', held collectively, constructs the edifice that is our deadened-down relating.

It is the week before Christmas and at 5.30 a.m. we have gathered, my church, on the railway station platform to bring hot drinks to unknown commuters.

The sun is not yet up, and so we stand between two darknesses: the becoming and the going-to.

You are our 'neighbour': the word, I once heard, best translated 'the stranger closest to me'. We wondered how we could love you? And we thought of your tiredness, your shivers and pre-sunlit yawning. So in moon-sparkled air we pour out hot-wet blessings, remembrances of home.

And you receive, eyes streaming earliness and cold as you tremble to armour yourself with lipstick; you receive, with clasping chapped hands, exhausted because your child has cried all night.

And you smile. Tiny muscles shift and we are human. As well as human, neighbours: dwellers in the same net of streets. We've lived side by side for years. You'd never know it, as the rushing mass arrives, and streams a string of atoms down the line. Each lighting point stares into space, turned from its atomic neighbour as if to choose the night. Standing at right angles to life.

But this dense dumb ritual is given pierce by folly. A plump tea-bag breaks the spell of stranging night. As tea and coffee are passed around, the light sparks down from atom to atom and soon the plat-form is brilliant. Brilliant between two darknesses: the becoming and the going-to.

We long to help warm you back to life.

We have only to know that tiny things can quell. Because tremen-dous the power that thralls behind it all: and lights between two darknesses.

Questions for reflection

1 Can you think of a recent example in your life of a small event or encounter making a more considerable impact? Why was this possible?

2 This reflection, inspired by the experience of standing on a railway station platform before daybreak, speaks of 'the light' that lights 'between two darknesses: the becoming and the going-to.' What does this mean to you?

3 To serve free tea and coffee to our early morning commuters at our parish's railway station was an act of love that had impact for being counter-cultural: it hinged on the quietly scandalous, but profoundly Godly, act of giving *a gift*. We gave out no leaflets, to avoid the gift deteriorating into seeming advertising, and accepted no donations, again, to preserve the giftedness of the 'gift' by avoiding deterioration into the currency of transaction which is the bedrock of consumer culture. This allowed the gift to speak in purity: to convey its message of unconditional love. Our commuters were struck by these strange gestures!

What other counter-cultural 'signs' (such as giftedness) could you use to speak of God's kingdom – and why?

4 What small thing might you do, what small change might you make, in your everyday life, to signal – indeed, to help God incarnate – his coming kingdom?

A prayer for today

Giving God, you pour yourself out for your world: and you have not preserved this fullness of light for our life to come, but bring it, by your Spirit, to enflame our present. Come and pour yourself, we pray, into our today. And, in return, empower us in imagination and courage to pour ourselves away in loving kindness for others. Teach us how best to speak of you, which signs to use to best convey *your* meaning. Amen.

(The) One

———◆———

Our pop songs talk endlessly of 'love'. But what are they preaching to us? With what are they filling our heads and our hearts? And what has the God revealed as Jesus Christ to say to us about the dangers and dizziness caused by certain interpretations of the passions he has set to light? How do we find a guide – to love?

*   *   *

Contemporary films, and romantic popular media, offer little in the education of love. In the (disparagingly and sexist-termed) 'chick-lit' genre, women (and men?) are offered a dominant narrative of 'the search for *the One*' that culminates in discovering the person who 'completes' *me*. A popular song at the time of writing celebrates with poppy verve a man's having found a 'cheerleader', who 'is always right there when I need her', who gives me what I want, whose presence guarantees the satiation of my particular desires, needs and hopes. She must be 'the One'.

The consummative points of such songs, films and novels seem innocent enough, but their truncated narratives precipitate at least a crisis in imagination, if not in practice, as human beings attempting to live by this pedagogy of desire wonder what the hell has gone wrong when life is not all climax. You do not satisfy me (that is, me *deeply*). You cannot be 'the One'.

What to do?

What of falling in love post-wedding day? Is it time to have an affair, as my need for being known, for being gazed upon with love, out-measures the stretch of your fragile, human heart: as much in need of gazing as my own?

Options, apparently, include separation, divorce and unfaithfulness.
A solicitor tells me that as a family lawyer he has become (literally)
depressed by the number of people seeking separation without any
recourse to reflection on relationship. To mirror, and realize, the cultural pedagogy, imagination fails.

But as we toss in our hot, fraught bed, we'd do well to wonder who
we're wrestling with.

'When it comes to God,' a spiritual guide informs me, 'we are deal-
ing with a lover.' If we are made by love, to pursue love, to come
home to (and by) love, this beguilingly simple recipe holds the key
to understanding the devastation of our tortured hearts. Already
half-betrothed, our forgetting selves plunge and dive at other bodies, making so-called loves that, even *at best*, court strange little
unfaithfulnesses. To this irony of life, this romantic tragedy, we are
all born actors, spending out to find the love(r) who already holds
us: there for vision were we but to turn, and learn the meaning of our
yearnings – source and seal.

I don't mean we're necessarily to be celibate. Rather (perhaps we're
not imaginative *enough*), we're all in a threesome: him; you, caller
for distinctive love; creation. Though not as our impoverished versions, written out of (and pain-embossing) disappointment, failure
of focus, distorted and shifting presence: and boredom, something to
spice up the void that is our self-narrative's ending.

As ever, God arrives where our narrative runs out. As death begins
her strange deranging tidying, he comes, and with understanding we
rarely give him credit for. 'Right love: wrong target.' And there *is* a
target, and there are flaming arrows too, your rucksack's full of them:
and they'll be burning holes in *you* unless you learn to fire them.

So as our pop songs propagate the myth of 'my One', finishing and
completing *me*, comes instead this awakening that our deepest yearnings point to wants less met.

There is You, and Me, and this Other who refuses to die in the heart
of our love-making, resisting exhaustion, but posited in every clue

that marriage is for making out God's love. This self-pouring makes its sense in tracing out in arcs what's coming, filling, from elsewhere as much as here, between us now.

But this is not a way our novels, films and pop songs tell. An author I admire reflects that we often seek God in libraries and classrooms: meanwhile, he's heading straight for the bedroom.[9]

What will it mean for you to meet your lover there?

Questions for reflection

1 It is no small thing to doom much of a generation to the imaginative impoverishment of being only able to conceive loving as self-gratification, as a combination of personal survival and received pleasure.

  What might the long-term penalties be for the in-forming of young imaginations through the contemporary mass-media? What kinds of anti-gospels are we preaching (consciously or unconsciously) through these routes?

2 In the Ignatian tradition, desire is often a key to locating God's calling in us, and to us. There is always need for a 'discernment of spirits' – to consider which desires will lead us to God, and which will lead us away from him – but growing intimacy with Jesus and a coming to understand his calling on our life begins with holding our desires before him in prayer, and learning to 'read' where God is breathing through their heat.

  How does this approach to spiritual discernment strike you? Are you aware that God has spoken to you, or is speaking to you, through your desires? Why do you think that desires may be a key to discovering God's relationship with us, and his aspiration for our lives?

3 What do you believe our culture currently says to us concerning love? Where have you seen what it says? Can you glimpse any opportunities to engage the culture about its assumptions and aspirations?

4 Where do you see the love of God pressing into this world, and in-spiring transformation into Christlikeness?

A prayer for today

Lord, many of us live lives of anxious frustration. We are educated by the voices and agendas of culture, and through the tools of mass media. Perhaps it has never been so important that we ask you for clearness of vision – for reality of perception – for the steadiness of that contemplative gaze which is able to 'discern between spirits', between helpful and less helpful urges and desires. Lend us the determination to rest in you, and to gaze on you: so that we will return to the world able to see what is of you, and what is not of you. And strengthen this muscle of inner vision, we ask, so that, seeing you more clearly, we will know where we are called to make the protest. Amen.

Graffiti

Romans 8.22–25

I am struck – as I travel through the world – by the ways I see the pains and achings of the culture make their protest all around me. On a prayer walk in our parishes, or driving home from a working weekend, I notice how literally the agonies are 'out there': painted on a banner in a field, scrawled across a broken-up building that no one can get access to. There is a deeper meaning that is coming to the surface of these planes: real voices make their protests on the fractured surfaces of our culture. Have you heard them? Have you discovered their sources? What is the culture crying?

* * *

Check the walls.

They show the spit of protest.

It was a vivid week. The world came pressing back to centre, singing out from its edges a single, desolate song: its song of Without You.

I'm driving on a major motorway, calculating across the fluster of five co-weaving lanes, when from the sideline calm of a field, almost out of view, a stretching line of paint spilt on brick announces: 'NOTHING IS PERMANENT'.

We continue striving angrily up our separate lanes. 70 . . . 80 miles per hour . . .

Cry from the sideline.

Graffiti

Some friends and I make a prayer walk through our parish. We're stopping here, pausing there, and praying: at a bus stop, a block of flats, the railway station, the local grocery shop – where myriad atoms unknown to us board trains, read papers, consume, and buy, make love and die. We're stopping here and there to hold the fleeting lives in everlasting arms: to call the veil that's shown itself as breathing under life to light these lives – that they might know the named one. And as we course the boundary of a field of wreckage, our selves barred out by crumbling walls, an opening gives just space enough to see scrawled in bleeding paint the banner – 'HOPELESS' – running under smashed-out windows, cut short where the carcass splits, collapsed beneath its heaving steel-spun skeleton. We pray: this place of agony, this place of ruin and ripping, sealed with riven walls.

Cry from the centre.

I'm walking through this vast shopping centre, when I realize I course beside a long and winding queue. Eventually I'm nearing what they're gathered for, passive, bored, obedient, with stares of dull oblivion. Only, here's a clashing fuss: a stationed team of clapping shop assistants, lined up inside the pristine store like death's own bridesmaids, cheering, shouting, carousing in tones of spectral celebration, 'Come in! It's time! Your phone's arrived! It's time! The new one's arrived!' And as I watch the first customer nervously enter the sanctuary beckoned by these white-shirted ghosts, I note how hungrily we gulp the pagan festival, even as we stand dying.

Cry from our stomachs.

It was a vivid week. Our spat cries: spitting from the sidelines, spitting from the centre, spitting from our gut-ties. Spit that lines the cry to leave on all our walls the shadows of our protest.

Come, directing one. Come the one so spat on. Come the one whose Being to the carcass-crack was full self-rendered. Come the one who's fulsome cried the scream of crucifixion.

Come the one who – body raised – poured out what comes to kiss with spit what cries as earthly cracked-up.

Come the one who *is* poured out: who rushes to the paling edge, and crumbling haunt – the fear I force away to edge, the abandoning within. Come the one who, while I flee, is bleeding out to edge and centre what is pouring on the cry: the one whose crying out to us is crucifixion's single antidote.

Questions for reflection

1 What urgent cry do you hear coming from the world around you today? *Look at me! I'm important, I'm significant, I matter.*

2 Where do you most recognize the world's need for the incoming of God's kingdom? What does the kingdom bring in these places? *In Government ???*

3 How would you put into words the deepest achings, the deepest desolations, of our culture? Can you offer these as the prayers of our culture to our God?

4 This reflection focuses on the places 'stuck' in Gethsemane, and in crucifixion, in the world immediately around us. What does this mean to you? How do you understand this? Where do you see this happening in your everyday life?

it means the word has not understood the Gospel message

5 The Italian Roman Catholic priest Raniero Cantalamessa writes that 'In the strictest sense, to create means to draw forth being out of nothingness'[10] (to create *ex nihilo* (from nothing), as Christian tradition espouses). Christian tradition also often interprets the encroachment of evil (which is not a positive presence, but a negating absence, a *privation* of being and goodness) as the collapse of creation, its regression, back towards this 'nothingness' again: back towards the nothingness and chaos from which it emerges, and against which God has spoken his decisive 'No' in Christ's resurrection.

In disagreement for the sake of – Power hungry. – Destructive

Where, in the culture around you, do you see this draw – this drain – to nothingness?

6 How can you help God's Spirit to bring healing?

A prayer for today

Lord, we see your world suspended in crucifixion where it protests out its agony in its divorce from its own realization and perfection. This is the alienation of sin. We pray for the world's redemption: that you would come, by your Spirit, and continue to love up into restored life, health and wholeness what is waiting for your promised future. Come, Holy Spirit. And bring your creation into Christ. Though we are already created beings, let us experience our re-creation. Amen.

Inarticulate
1 Corinthians 15.1–11

One of the most unnerving experiences I have had in parish ministry was when invited to give the 'talk' at a local secondary school's Christmas assembly.

I arrived to find the service being prepared, and ending rehearsal, in the hall (and it was to repeat several times, so large was the school). There was the usual bifurcation of those students already well in residence in orchestra or choir, and those masses arriving noisily into hassled rows, with every sinew protesting their refusal to be tamed for long – like a warning.

I was uneasy as I witnessed, from my singularly still spot, this pre-service presentation before the summoned order. And I realized the reason: for the ageless bifurcation, what was entirely shared was a kind of listless misery. Teachers, stressing and fussing at manuscripts, and hauling lines of children, had closed-up faces that were fed up and harried, eyes down-averted; the carolling crowds had no desire to be here; and even the apparently invested instrumentalists and choristers looked out glazily on the amassing congregation without anticipation or recognition. In sterling irony, this festival dedication to the divine life's hospitality in hosting us, and its seasonal call to humanity to contemplate their heart's returning hospitality of him, glinted cold and desolate behind rejecting facades and barely warmed metal instruments.

Nobody said 'Hello'.

Realizing I was thirsty, I tried to find the staff room to get some water. Outside, in a ubiquitous grey corridor, a teacher pointed the way but did not take me there. Upstairs, finding the labelled 'staff room', I walked into a space (myself an oddity in clerical collar) and arrived lost in a clearing of beige carpet while groups of teachers clustered possessively round the sidelines. Several looked up, then down, re-closing the circle. I found the water cooler myself, filled a flimsy paper cup, and then returned to the Assembly Hall below, taking my plastic seat in the otherwise abdicated front row.

I was invited to give the talk – and had chosen, and never had it seemed more required or timely, to remind the school of the reason for this coming Christ-mass.

But before I spoke it was the particular, and clearly significant, role of one teacher, as representative of the life of the school, to contribute a poignant seasonal reflection: a lesson to the children, a distilled wisdom. 'What is Christmas all about?' was the forecasted heart of his message-to-come. And then a man as sad, as strangely clad in eerie passivity, as the extending room stood up to share with us how one Christmas his grandmother, who had been with them the previous year, was now dead and lost to him. He had never had the chance to say goodbye. Christmas is now a sorry memory of his lost opportunity. 'My advice to you', he continued to the thousand assembled mute faces, 'is to make Christmas a time to remember that family is precious because one day they're not going to be there.' (Festal angel.) 'In a way, then,' he flourished, 'Christmas for me has been about saying goodbye.' The tinsel shivering on the lectern beneath his breath seemed specially unmeaning.

The choir stood to sing a secular song – granted, to remind us of those less comforted than ourselves this Christmas. But I couldn't help considering that this solemn contribution was their paean singularly worked on, their many weeks' meditation: and the chanting plea to 'wake me up when it's all over' reverberated about the room, tackling several tangents and mirroring a variety of assembled emotions.

Amid all this, and in consistent spirit, we intermittently sang our Christmas carols, yes. The choir stood, the orchestra bent, the conductor joylessly gesticulated, the congregation grumpily stood (or refused to stand, for we were now 20 minutes in), to sing and play by rota and by rote these remembered strangelings. These chanted collections of 'Thees' and 'Thous' and 'ivys' and 'shepherds' and 'bells' and 'child' and 'star' and 'manger' were spun out with all the flat fate of dead symbol. Stranger still was the act of announcing such advice as 'Good Christian men rejoice' as every imperative to take heart, to know comfort, to receive life was announced as though mortality had swallowed life again, and undone St Paul's hymnody.

And then came me: most weirdly centred sentinel, the one who at a Christmas celebration ought to have been most at home, yet now arrived erupting from the quarried bomb site, leaping from the earth-grave, the unexpected and protesting guest at some cultural ritual's funeral, embarrassing the thinning tinsel with bursts of actual light – not lent, but sourced.

'Christmas is *not* about "Goodbye"', I gently charged, with an apology to the teacher for renting his anti-gospel on home turf: 'Christmas is the greatest "Hello" in the whole of history.' And then I was scandalous: simply reminding this amnesia-d assembly – this strange, disordered, miserable, timeless creature, Postmodernity in person, towing his dissonant cacophony of inherited symbols with scruffy disinterestedness – that the point of their assembly, of this party they had poured their labour into, is the one called Jesus Christ. I could not register a response: they disappeared before me as the hall lights blasted headlong in my eyes.

With a nameless crunching in my gut, I took my lonely seat again. I wondered as the dumb liturgy crept on, swimming with the gathered hundreds of young faces, what they were being given to live for, to celebrate, through this wan remembering, the anaemic instruction of those they're looking up to.

Be one thing, or another, is one conviction: at least be loyal to the principles of education; if the commitment is to rejecting Christ, then leave aside the carolling and mirth. Set the landscape clearly: perceive all that's truly stripped away. And if you find your spirit pro-tests, seek integrity: and the meaning of your songs. For it strikes me that you don't know what you're doing: that you don't know what you're saying. This is not education. Neither is it integrity. Neither is it bread and water for living on. It's inarticulate, self-uncomprehending, strange pretending, breeding desolation crowned with plastic stars.

In the end, the released footsteps of several hundred children rampaged out, spinning their energy into a world we'd had a brief time to think about. I was not needed for the next service; someone else was coming in to speak. I wondered what they were going to preach. For, clearly, we're all preaching: even those posing 'neutral'.

So it was time to leave, and I did, walking out of the emptied hall, and as I crossed the stretching lawns could hear already the distant echo of corridors filled with restless streaming atoms.

I continued down the long driveway, suspended in the twilight chill of a late December night-day.

Nobody said 'Goodbye'.

Questions for reflection

1 Do you think our culture preaches an anti-gospel? If so, what does it contain? And what are its means of proclamation?

2 'For we're all preaching: even those posing "neutral" ': do you agree with this? What does it mean to you?

3 In the circumstance conveyed by the reflection, what would you have preached, and how? What were the distinctive challenges of the situation? Where, in such contexts as this, is there possibility and hope for a message of hope? Indeed, for a proclamation of the *promises* of God, captured in the gospel?

4 Where has our culture become inarticulate when it comes to preaching the gospel? What feels to have become unsayable, and why do you think this is so? How can you imagine the articulation – this evangelism, this telling of 'the good news' – being revived? How could you attempt it?

A prayer for today

Eternal and life-giving God, so much of our world – beneath the thin layers of tinsel – preaches desolation and strangely absurd comforts.

As we watch so much of our culture rejecting what it thinks it knows of you, and returning to crouch at the foot of the cross, comprehending its own wretchedness, we pray: come, by your Spirit, and bring your life. Come by the power of your resurrection, and revive our communities to sense, and meaning, and life again. We especially lift to you, beautiful Lord, those whose lives are lived from the pit of despair. Send your light. Amen.

Eclipse: full immersion
John 12.1–8
Mark 14.32–42

———————•◆•———————

Here is a low point. But a necessary low point.

I once had a friend who said, 'Perhaps we have to know hell before we can know heaven.' I had no idea what he meant – at the time. He was a mystic.

Sixteen years later, personal experience, an acquaintance with the writings of the Christian mystics that has given words to interpret that experience, and the pangs of continuing conversion as evermore unredeemed parts of myself are plunged into Christ's death before their rising, have shown that there is sense – inevitable sense – in this: the night is the gateway to life. Nicodemus comes to Jesus 'at night' to ask the most essential question of his existence (John 3). Perhaps it is merely indication that this reputable professional wanted to ask his questions of the strange Rabbi beneath the secrecy of shrouding darkness. But perhaps it also suggests, as the great pray-ers of Christian history testify, that it is through an inevitable desert experience, a crisis and loss of world-based certainties, that we are radically prepared for rebirth by God's own Spirit. There can be meaning in our suffering: it may be the way to transfiguration.

Much of our world is still hung in crucifixion: suspended in the night while what is won by Christ in principle awaits the Spirit's coming to enact and bring to life.

Where do you see this? Have you known times of despair to be strangely, even uniquely, fruitful? What did you learn?

* * *

All I see is sex and death:
mortals;
portals;

and whispered immortality.
I seize subconscious' bubbles as they rise:
you must decide
if all the Faith of youth is nothing worth,
is glistening beads of beauty hung on thread
condemned as web,
light-spun, then trembling, dead,
or else:

New Birth.

And a new tread,
that takes us dancing into Light
but leaves us to the earth as seeming mad,
though all their wisdom's now as madness' tortures turned.

So, gasping: Bread?

What new to eat
to wean this Light-started ewe from foot to head?

And here I'm turning back to pages
once seemed distant, jaded, faded,
dream-misted texts brought dusty out in Sunday school:
Yet – now – What? – When happened *this*?
Their words are flame-shine bladed,
slicing tightly 'Cross the frames of lifelines braided,
and Making Sense:
simple, clean, clear-stated,
more than making sense: the only life that's Life.

This is how it is.

These Scriptures spelling out
with ease unaided
what is blatant
all proportions flush, cascading
delivering, making manifest,
bewailing:
He is come:
and Earth is made with.

Oh healer, to my broken mind come rushing,
for I'm first-time full-time comprehending
wasteland living.
Begging to be living-waters-raided:
Come! – bring agony of understanding balm.

Be careful what you ask for.

To ask to know Reality
may bring you plunging into Hell's own waters
world-mind brought to die: 'fore it might Rise
now knowing true who made for.

Ruthless Spirit: He comes splicing flesh from bone
– yet what's in concepts known –
in wrecking false-stuck meanings making idols:

this stinking crucifixion in the Mind now homed
to make your Knowing womb for prophet-children.
Expect to bleed
as all your once-so-knowing comes undone.

Yet grasp the pain:
He is not Death –
strange-clothed deliverer –
but rather, death be-wielding
gives you second labour
though you're *knowing*
as Creator pulls you out, this time.

And Life's first cry?
For mind new-stunned same Way as for elsewhere,
– One Way, one Truth, one Life –
as when for body kneels with tears fell broken:
Turn around: and see the one who Raises
and take your long-fought jars of wealth
– the honeys bought to save you,
bought to praise you –
and new invest
and break them
o'er his feet
and weep

and wrap your hair with yearning
'fore a world un-comprehending
of your Madness
which is birthing Brilliance
as Thought makes love as well as flesh and heart.

It's dreadfully simple, you see.
The Law applied to Mind as elsewhere bent
– Die to Live –
fires new-bound birthing thoughts
to constellations wrought
shot-out from earth-fruit anchor:

Resurrection

Questions for reflection

1 This reflection conveys the absurdity of the world comprehended without Christ: and, therefore, the fresh vividness with which the gospel arrives when received amid the horror of life without God. Have you experienced something like this? Does the journey resonate?

2 How do you understand the baptism of our minds and imaginations?

3 Do you think that God's Spirit might grow us by plunging us into a 'dark night of the soul' – a time when certainties and settled places (often idols) are stripped away, and our truest motivations revealed and refined under pressure? How might you understand such a strange blessing?

4 Where are parts of your culture still hung in crucifixion, in a kind of agony? Where is the culture depressed? Lost? Fearful? What does healing look like in this context?

5 Our news reports, obsessively, on stories that incite fear: that keep us suspicious of the neighbour we are meant to be loving, locked down in isolated forms of deadened living, and intent on pursuing gospel-life's opposite; that is, focusing on preservation of self. Where have you recently seen this incitement of fear in the media? What stories are selected to create this consciousness? What *other* stories have we to tell – to testify?

A prayer for today

Lord, here is bloody honesty. The speared One, the nailed One, the tortured One, the flesh-spliced One: come in the exquisite tenderness of your eleventh-hour friendship, companion of crucified criminals.

Give us not more to bear, by your instigation Lord, than we can bear.

And when it comes to what comes not from you, deliver us from Nothingness. Haul us back to life – our only lifeline. Amen.

Night of fire
John 18.15–18, 25–27
John 21

━━━━◼◦◦◼━━━━

> The boy was like a corpse, so that most of them said, 'He is dead.'
> But Jesus took him by the hand and lifted him up, and he was able to
> stand.
>
> (Mark 9.26–27)

Is your heart broken?

Look again: what waits for hope in you? What dream, what question, what aspiration, what longing? What devastation knows the only hope is resurrection: something coming from beyond me to bring a dawn I'm never going to conjure from this pit? Dust only makes more dust: if I'm to live I need another life-source to be arriving from outside this sealed-off system. Do you know that feeling? That sense of looking at some fractured part of you and the certainty that nothing in me has power to heal this? It will need to be lit from elsewhere?

Because, you know: it *is* coming. And don't despise the dark. It was on the wastes of early morning fishing lakes that they realized something was burning on the shoreline – over *there*. And some lights are only visible at night time.

*   *   *

It starts in the dark.

(All life does. Nicodemus came by night.)

It is before the morning, and the early lights are yet to break through. This time – because it is a cosmos, not an earth-measured day that we speak of – there is no guarantee that anything comes quenching through the night. The prophesied sun's arrival merely comes to beg, to shadow-ask, if any true sun is coming from ahead, some promised orb, to light and shape and line the little, measured day: to set this wetted clay to something lasting.

And here, between the two great nights, we're at our work, our daily toil, to which the needs and rites of earth-life bend us all our life-long days. And Peter's curse is memory, deflating spirit with every re-turning thought that casts to courtyards where love ended, as, of course, it does, at the edges of blood-letting. All life's climax.

We're back at work. Reliable drudgery, and catching nothing: catching Nothing. Our eyes, night-weary and bleared with all our sighing, drift aft across the interminable surface – where all is plane – to hover down there on the shoreline.

But the pearly stretch – the shore that is both launch and homing port for this naught-catching boat – lies not so dimly under Night-evening's mists.

For night's retiring. And the planeing line, which rested horizontal, is crossed with fire that flies into the sky while spearing down the water almost to our boat.

All dimensions are invested.

And what would this be? But aesthetic consolation if it weren't that this arising light is personed: for *he* comes to us in early fires. This coming, willing, bodied one, who lets us kill him *knowing* we can't live like this: lights out. So as we float adrift within the flattened world of murdered yearning, having done our worst and flat denied what One contests our own divining, it's the friend we've sliced who's coming down to light a fire at that approaching edge where all our Nothingness is lapping. Blessed encroachment, this, who draws his line at our dissolving: firming earth.

And, more, he calls me 'friend'; and he asks about my trouble (why I catch nothing, and persist in catching Nothing); and he points the way to life as I now cast my nets to his inviting, seeing this is killing death: to learn to cast my life with Life's aligning.

For the Night is out.

The shores are fired.

And all new life's fires stoked: and not with invisibles and abstractions, some purely metaphysical assurance (though these logical constellations know the reordering too), but, this morning, with a fleshly friend who is calling from the flotsam fireside, 'Come and have breakfast, loved one.'

And I come – come to the second fire, which, as I near, reveals itself as nourished by the one who's lending light. And second fire it is, for here's an echo of one earlier met: I've warmed like this before, not on a shore, but in a courtyard, where I played my part to spin the net that caught you up and cursed our catches thence to spreading nets in nothingness, to endless drift in spilt-out oceans.

And so – sore-knowing this – you build a fire, from all this twisted, blistered wreck, and call me to your side to see how life's first fire is come to serve what second lights, and, lighting, burns away what pains and starts again with asking: 'Do you love me?' Ever life's behest. To coming home.

And what love is this? For it's not passing care, or sparking lust, or bright affection, but would wind my will as well: in some new bondage? Yes, *sweet* bondage, for this is no lighting up of some fair-set pair, due to burn to dust, but is the life that lets and loves what's made while setting it to glory.

So my prayer is that you'll light me up: that I become the fire as well, source-lit by him who comes as burning bush (that bush, remember, though burning was not consumed) to tell that he who spirit-lights is blessing flesh as well. For breaking bread's to share with all that morning's breakfast, yet to come, will find us, gathered, lit by Life, refined to matter's shining.

Questions for reflection

1 What does it mean, to you, to be baptized into the death of Jesus Christ, and to be born again into his risen life?

2 Have you experienced a 'night of fire'?

3 Where has resurrection happened in your life?

4 'We're back at work. Reliable drudgery, and catching nothing: catching Nothing.' Where do you see people struggling with work that feels meaningless? What does it look like for people to engage, instead, with meaning-full work? What do you think this reveals about God's purposes for his creation?

5 What, in our culture (its values or goals), rests on the assumption of the finality of finitude and mortality? Does this give parts of our culture – such as advertising – certain powers?

6 Which aspects of our culture would be contested by a realization of the everlasting life that comes by participating in Christ's resurrection? What – and who – would be set free?

A prayer for today

Lord, do not leave us cleaving to the cross. When we haven't the strength to stand again, haul us up like those glimmering nets, caught up in the promise of your Son. Lord, when I am most lost, most despairing, most cast out to sea, let me hear you calling from the shoreline, calling me to breakfast: as your friend. Be my restoration – One who is living on the other side of death, the wilds behind him. By your Spirit, and our working with you, bring the world to shore. Amen.

Lifted
Matthew 14.22–36

A revelation, a new awareness, a clarity, came to me while running on the treadmill at the gym. Know the feeling? It was while I was consumed in something else and my mind was running free that I felt arriving over me with the fullness of a world (less a theory or a thought) the conviction that it's *as we run out* that God gets to raise us. And it's delicious! Sensing that, as I send my being flying across this running machine towards its inevitable collapse, there is someone waiting to catch and chuck up into the air my final flat-out self.

Do you have a sense of where your limits lie? And what is made possible by your reaching them? If, despite all our anxious activity to create, sustain and save ourselves, we need only to rest and wait to receive our life that comes by the grace of God, then what are you set free from? And let's go cosmic (for it *is*): what is the world set free from? Why are we running?

*   *   *

We reach our end, I am run out:
and fainting flat
all self-faith spent,
self-saving rent,
am floored to find
then comes a heave:
but not in sinew,
rather as the earth's womb wrested weight,
churns rolling over,
kneading flesh:

we wait.

Making love works best if both arcs bend
to blend
and so, in meeting, kissing then befriend:
so does creation to God tend
to meet his bend
once full-begotten
now once-done, extend:

– and then, like lovers' bodies weaved,
this holy tangle
earth rises but to find the weight of heaven
pressing down with weighty kiss
already arriving
God is Spirit
Life is Spirit
Kiss is Spirit
receive, and rise,
and damn the earth-hewn politics that fights surrender, protesting life's all fight;
Behold the night:
and naked
become pregnant with the Spirit's laying seed
receive your Life
as giving birth to life is birthing you.

And now is sinew rescued too
as promises on promises come falling, pressing through
each pre-ceived limit
calling: 'Yet!'

He used the bread and wine to show
that fruit of earth and star-dust now
he'll strike to Life
but – then – to Glow
with his own Life reloaded.

So, as he walks on water there,
I utter from the earth my prayer,
'Call me to you – it's yours to Rise
this dust to bridal nights.'

Questions for reflection

1 Have you felt you grasped something extraordinary, had a revelation about God's nature or plan, in the middle of something very ordinary? What does this possibility reveal?

2 Where do you see *the world around you* 'lifted' into new life? Lifted in a way it could not muster for itself (no more than the creature can enact his or her own resurrection)?

3 'Making love works best if both arcs bend/ to blend/ and so, in meeting, kissing then befriend': do you feel called to help a particular part of the world around you – a particular aspect of culture – move towards the tender befriending gesture of its maker?

4 What, in the culture around you, 'fights surrender' to the kingdom's arrival and reign?

5 What has the power of the Riser God made you pregnant with? What does he teach you in the night?

A prayer for today

Lord, with such passion you have won us: this tender passion. And we yearn to return this love you lend, undoing Judas' kiss. This return is nature's revival. As we brace at the shock of contact – the shock of your promise to our very flesh – teach us who we are now in this rising: our diviner and definer, as we realize it is not who I am, but only who I am *as raised in you* that's (literally) mattering. Amen.

Wrecking ball
Luke 15.11–32

———◄•►———

The dog waits. She waits, consumed with one thought. When will he come home? Her eyes are clear, shining, steady on the door handle: waiting for a sign, a hint of shift in the air's direction, something to mark the way of the loved one's intention. She is full, forward-facing, anticipating, adoration. When is he coming home?

*

A friend of mine recently spoke about his relationship with his two daughters. He is a professional man with a demanding job and was relating how tirelessly the phone rings with business calls all day, how many hours of the day are spent in unmissable meetings with high-octane clients. His working space is the epitome of a high-pressure environment. 'But,' he added, 'there is one call I will always take, no matter what is happening in the office, no matter who I'm in a conference with. That's if one of my daughters rings.'

He went on to explain that his daughters are different in character. Frequently he will work his long hours from home, where he has a study in the heart of the house. One of his daughters, he said, the younger, is a spirited, tempestuous, confident girl, who thinks nothing of barging with gusto into her father's office when she wants to speak with him or merely to have his attention for a while. His second daughter, the elder, is more timid: moreover, she has suffered, and her cautious manners, hesitations and retreats are clues to a bruising in her spirit that she has entrusted to few but her father, and he knows what the signs betoken. She will knock quietly at the door, so tentatively it is easy to miss her, and then, when invited in, steps only in one foot, still hovering on the threshold and whispering out apologies for disturbing him.

As the father works in his office day by day, and receives the varying approaches of his daughters, his heart begins to fold around one desire. He lifts his head, takes off his glasses, looks at us and says, 'Honestly, what I would give to have my elder girl breaking the door down to get to me whenever she needs me, like my youngest does.'

*

There is a painting in Liverpool Cathedral that depicts that well-known (perhaps less well-grasped) parable often named (though it's to catch but one resonance) 'The Prodigal Son'. A father who has waited long for his estranged son to come home recognizes an approaching frame. He has watched, for years, a horizon the emptiness of which declares the lost son's freedom to decide where he belongs. But now, today, a desolate, home-hungry figure, bent with exhaustion as spiritual as physical, approaches on the way that leads to where he's known and loved without condition. The father is already – has always been – on his feet, on the way, looking out for the boy who forgot his origin, and the yearning of his heart pours out in active, outstretched arms. The son had but to turn, had but to lean his eyes this way, to bring his watchful father running down the road to meet him: this son who comes home towing with him all the painted background, vast creation, as a spreading gold-flecked cloak.

The painting – to one who has read Jesus' parable of 'The Running Father', or 'The Prodigal Father' (for to be 'prodigal' is to give to the point of reckless ruin) – is a familiar scene. But one character is unexpected. He (or she?) is also sufficiently small to be missed, or glossed by passing vision as incidental, or passed over as a sentimental touch, or dismissed as an ornamental detail, as our lazy eyes latch on to what's familiar, even domesticized. For the father's reaching arms, though determined, have not yet caught hold of the shoulders of his homing son: and between them both, springing from the feet of the father, and making contact through his paws with the legs of the son, is a small dog. He – she – stands in the gap: in the gap between the father and the son; between home and the turning creation.

The little dog leaps.

Between the familiar vision of the arriving father and the familiar bent of the returning son is this sparky little ball of darting energy: and the painter's genius is found in feeling the urgent, passioned press of her paws on your own knees.

Anyone who has had a dog run at them to greet them as they come home knows this welcome: determined, unashamed, single-hearted, focused, unselfconscious, a consuming desire to get to you. I am sure the painter wants us to *feel* the homecoming: beyond the threatened familiarity of beholding stale imagery, the sterile angles of intellection, to sense *tangibly* the press brought down on flesh by this wild life, by her reaching, probing claws.

Here is Jesus' picture of creation returning to its maker; of an individual returning to their heavenly Father; of the Gentiles – and those who come last, least and latest – brought wholeheartedly into God's abundant life; of Jesus' own incarnate, spent-out, frame raised and ascended into the eternal triune life of God. The first, second and third meanings are made possible by the fourth. But in this little dog we have specially foregrounded, perhaps, the love that leaps towards the world with Spirit's bounding press. Her frame bursts with the Father's own love as, gathering the Son home, she presses through him – and thereby out! – into all creation.

*

The dog waits. She waits, consumed with one thought. When will you come home? Her eyes are clear, shining, steady on the door handle: waiting for a sign, a hint of shift in the air's direction, something to mark the way of your cherished intention. She is full, forward-facing, anticipating, adoration. She is often disrespected, her love seems scruffy, reckless, pathetic, needful, easy to ridicule, to call insubstantial, in a world that so fears its own weakness.

Love waits. Love waits, consumed by one thought.

When are you coming home?

Questions for reflection

1 What is this reflection saying to you today?

2 Where have you experienced a person's passionate yearning to get home to the Father – either your own yearning, or someone else's?

3 Where have you recently seen a part of the world yearning to be home with the Father? Yearning for well-being, restoration, acceptance, peace and the simple knowing that I am, and always will be, loved?

4 What does the term 'reconciliation' mean to you?

5 Our culture so often presents feeling need, dependence – such as feeling the need to belong – as weakness. This sets us up at right angles to the most significant needs of the human heart, to the most vital constellating of the cosmos – to Christ. It frustrates our ability to receive God's pursuit of us as the finite creatures we are. Instead, we make, or receive, our idols: our pretending possessions of sufficiency.

Where do you notice this tension?

A prayer for today

Running Father, one with the power and speed to course the stars, you have defined your own freedom as the love that scoops the Son to win us home. Have us coming home within Christ's cloak, creation gold-crowned trailing in his jewel-stepped stead. One who has granted out to have the Son back only with us towing, teach us to love *as that love* that lives between the Father and the Son, so that this love may be pouring out of us into this turning world. Amen.

Radical

John 14.5–7

Our world is rightly cautious about what it calls 'religious extremism'.
But what space remains to articulate the possibility of a revelation
that is distinctive and available to all?

As postmodernism imbues popular culture with the self-defeating
conviction that there is no absolute truth, except the absolute truth
that there is no absolute truth, where does that leave the claims of
faith? Or, rather, putting it the other way round: how do the revealed
claims of faith interrogate your culture's current approach to ideas of
truth? How do *you* speak into this challenge?

This poem seeks to capture the simplicity – and the contention –
of the Christian's situation, endeavouring to show how the distinc-
tiveness of Christ's way to the Father is precisely *not* excluding in its
availability to all.

*   *   *

One way out,
One way through –
Held to you.

Read as closed,
Protested 'old' –
Distortion.

Claimed unfair,
'Intolerant':
Now's religion.

Coming to you,
Absolute, True:
Odd? But Facted.

We're not writing,
We're the written – strange submission, yet:
Beholden.

One way out,
One way through –
Here for you.

Life's been made through –
Life's being shaped through –
Life's being kept through –

This is golden.

He's to own It –
He's to crown It –
Thirsty?

Here's as God is.
Here's as God is.
God's as God is: spoken.

Jesus Christ:
the Lord, the Life, the Lasting,
open to you –

Come.

Questions for reflection

We live in an age of religious pluralism. It is highly unfashionable, in places even dangerous, to claim that one religion represents a distinctive and unique way to God. Christ's way to the Father is precisely *not* excluding because it is available to all. However, when religions are (falsely) interpreted as competing systems of truth-claims, as if we were choosing between different games to play, it becomes very hard for people to see how one faith might be both distinctive and universally available. The first misunderstanding, of treating religions in ways incompatible with their nature, has been fatal. A whole possibility has become invisible: the possibility that one way might be the way for everyone in a manner that satisfies both the facted-ness of a unique revelation in history and the pluralist's admirable desire to embrace everyone in value.

1   How does your culture interpret or receive distinctive claims about the meaning of life, or worthwhile ways of living life?

2   The gospel confronts the finite creature with the facts of life: the shape of existence and its promised End. What endures is what is conformed to Christ – what lives *in him* – the one to shape the End, who *is* the End. Christ *is* Omega – he is everything's destiny. If you want to see the future, the ultimate future, look at Jesus.

   Where does the world in which you live and move and have your being receive this news? What are the signs?

   Where does the same world struggle to accommodate this revelation? What are the signs?

A prayer for today

Lord, your work on our behalf is sufficient, full-bodied, facted. The only remaining work for us is to believe in the one you have sent – your Son, Jesus Christ – and to live the lives that come flowing out of this first faith. Speak to us of your sufficiency; the power of your grace. Help us to speak to our culture of your sufficiency; and the power of your grace. We pray that, as your Spirit goes before us in this, hearts and minds are prepared – in a realization that surpasses false assumptions – to relinquish what is so often seen as the exclusivity of a stricture: and to see, in its place, the open well and welcome gate: One who is Way to the Father. Amen.

Our Father

Some routes to God are surprising – even painful. It may be a realistic encounter with limitation and loss that shocks us into the kind of availability of heart that makes it easier for God to arrive to us, and for us to realize that he is, indeed, all in all.

In this reflection, I consider how the thought of losing my own dad in the future – whom I love – already throws a shadow over the present. Life often holds such shudders. These facts are lodged in the heart of life for all of us. But can loss become a pointer? Can it become a pointer to what remains?

*   *   *

They say it's harder
to come by the Father
if you never had a good one.
His Goodness is then faith's fable,
the Impediment rendering unstable
what else may come that Way.

But no one speaks of what's to make of
Fathers good:
such as the one
who me-begot
who me love-knotted into life
yet shows all dust-life's tending?

Of what's to do when earthing's Father
– anchored all –
yet starts to wane t'ward sleep
with new-greyed protest?

Of what's to do when what's required
is not some sweet conversion out of early pain to learn to trust,
but rather,
having grown in safety,
now,
in ripening years,
new tremors own?

Where's now – Who's now – my God? And . . . father?

I see how corrupt, or absent, father, sources the Imagination's fail:

but deep, too, desolations lie
as Firmaments crack dry with pale of age
and towers topple down
on Father's princess: stating 'waste'
and blasting dreamt-of kingdoms
sung 'fore sleep.

Another idol? Clue: that even love seems yielding out to
passing Time's cruel crunch on earthly byways.

But someone's watching:

For the Son,
pressing loving deeper,
subsides only enough to let my vision
fall beyond his face to spy another measure:

Underneath: the everlasting arms
with Father's broad-soft palms,
with might to crush,
wait stretched for cuddling up
his heart-crunched princess
brought to chest for kisses:
Godhead's seed.

Our Father: for, through words said from near birth
I find – for first time now – that Dad you are
(He *did* say: cry to 'Abba'):
and revealed here is:
Eternity is tender:

pulsing out through care-carved darkness
what is born to need to home.

Yet, see: returning (what's actually first-homing)
is a midlife's lesson in first-learning:
for eternal Father shows the holy destiny of earth-dust ones
with whom he shared his children's care,
as father's earth-love pours out Everlove's refractions.

Questions for reflection

1 Where have you experienced loss in your life? What shapes can loss take?

2 What are the losses that haunt our culture? Where do we see their shadowing signs? (Think not only of people, but of more abstract, yet nevertheless endemic, losses: such as loss of youthfulness, which our culture struggles to grieve and therefore continually endeavours to evade.)

3 Does our culture articulate loss? Are there forms of bereavement it finds more difficult to capture/articulate? Why? What is the consequence of the lack of grieving/evasion? Which losses does our culture repress?

4 What is the consolation of the gospel for our culture's spiritual sites of bereavement, loss and longing?

A prayer for today

Son of God and Son of Man, with playful, intimate spirit you called your Father in heaven 'Daddy'. Your Spirit who lives with us, on 'our side' of our prayer, empowers us to call God 'Father', as the adopted children we are. As we raise our eyes to the one we need to know remains, let your Spirit be praying perfectly, in our depths, what we cannot find the words to say, what we do not even know to name: for grief, for pain, for bewilderment, for not-knowing what, for all our loss in sighing. Continue to send your Spirit into the whole world, with this hidden prayer that sees the secret places. May the prayer of our culture come to echo what is prayed for it by your healer-Son. May we know ourselves beholden in the desert middling hours. Amen.

Blow

Acts 2.1–21

We've all had 'one of those days': when we end the day spent with exhaustion. In the early weeks of a new job, a particularly hectic time brought me home feeling torn to pieces. But as I began to reflect over the day, I realized how much of the battle was caused by my simply trying to control everything and to appear a certain way. Indeed, as I began to look again more carefully over the hours, I started to see how much divine life had been arriving, and I found myself grieving for what I'd missed as I warred on in the fray. Here, I realized, was a calling: to sit with time and events differently, and so to be free to be attentive to what God is weaving through the day. But I had to use other eyes: eyes not intent on seeking ways to control events and remain 'Queen' of my life, but eyes content to search for the Spirit's movements . . . a whole new tuning.

*   *   *

It was one of *those* days. It ends with melting eyes blearing from hours' watching under brilliant lights, and a mind frenzied-out to frazzling by questions dropped to my feet like falling marbles, scattered for me to slip on, dripping out far quicker than I can capture, lay hands or mind or eyes on . . .

It was one of *those* days. I'm called to hold my poise from start to end like some suspension bridge while underneath the bombs (whose only consistency is exploding with regularity) are spitting up the soil:

> It's the session I forgot to plan,
> the unexpected call to present,
> the pitch that flails from anxiety,
> the unplanned room change,

91

the memory stick forgotten at home,
the cog that broke,
the bit of system that choked,
the message that failed delivery consigning to 'Draft' what was
meant to crown the day:
    Pronouncement: just so, I'm binned as Queen . . .

It was one of *those* days that sends you out reeling: the bridge-base
cracked from surfacing booms, as little fires spark-up in myriad
places 'I' am far from fine.

It's out!
That *I* do not perform so fair;
and *I* do not control so well;
and I show out, hot-glistening care,
all out for you to walk on.

And,
worst of all,
I cannot fight the fires so quick
to hide their glare's arrival in my starting eyes,
and as the sun sets down on crumbling brick
the day-wrung wreck has only life to say
'thank God for the end of one of *those* days.'

But rest comes.

Overnight the perfumes of dream and prayer and Scripture mingle.
And by the morning light has spoken out:
it comes with clarity:
'behold *my* days among you: note their patterning'.

So I look again
at the start of Christ's own ministry
to find that in the space of a page
– as if in a day –
is the announcing slam of the prophet's imprisonment,
the high-blessing of baptism outpouring love,
the hurling to wilderness,
the love-filled, love-stirred leaning into Godbreast-pressing
crowds

and then retreat into the dark and silence that shoulders life before the birthing of new-day.

It's high
and low
and high
and low
that throws out to flat-lateral only our assumption that his coming shall be marked by this world's peace: both the land of inward fires and our outward world of structures, rules and acts.

So with this frame, I gaze again on broken, exhausted Yesterday.

And it's differently:

I see what came to break the frame, I spot the sparks that lit the bombs, bright omens that I shock to see had melted to invisible as I was overcome with sweating self. What I had cast out to the edge – encounters noted but so soon pressed back, destined to invisibility by my own blindness – come rushing up into the space new-vacated as the bulbous clouds of thundering dust, of 'I', begin to dissipate.

And now I see what has arrived:
the creatures who have graced my day:
the seeker from another world asking out her questings, eyes all-longing, rising bright with all she's fought to come and study, this full Life she knows;
the full-sweep tide of ministers, cloud of witnesses, arrived upon a threshold as they dedicate their serving to their Love.
Within my day's breaking was the coming of this life –
that I see now –
and that the chaos and the turmoil here is only our nets breaking as the bounty of the Lover's love comes crackling into Now.

And *heave.*

This God does not bring chaos:
this Spirit broods to massage into order all into life's Frame,
yes: Christ.

Christening culture.
Christening creation.

But all our best-worn ways find themselves rough split,
and our selves crest-tossed,
as that simplifying, ordering life arrives – its course to rearrange us.

And I am cracked to life: as birthing Spirit rises from behind the
veil to press to centre what arrives by rupture.

Blessed rupture.

Questions for reflection

1 Have you recently had a day when something pressed for your
attention by disordering you?

2 Have you recently 'missed' the reordering Spirit's arrival – mis-
taking it for something else?

3 When the kingdom comes, it often turns the world on its head:
it may do the same to us and our priorities and habits! Have you
discovered this recently?

4 How does your culture feel about, interpret, respond to, order
and disorder? Capability and incapability? Control and surrender? Does its attitude to these ways of being affect its capacity to
understand the nature of the kingdom of God – and that kingdom's servants?

5 How could you help the culture in which you 'live and move and
have [y]our being' (see Acts 17.28) be more alert to, and responsive
to, the work of the Holy Spirit?

6 What, in your culture, is set to be strained by Life's arrival? Where
are you, and those around you, in danger of resisting the kingdom's coming because it would upset a status quo? What would be
signs of the kingdom coming as contest?

A prayer for today

Lord, when we are missing you, teach us to look again and see the
seeker. The Spirit is a verb-al life: teach us to be prepared for rearran-
ging – and not to resist it, when it's you who's coming through, as
heaven through earth. The cross is a crux, spending out to pull life
back to order. Help us to be readers of divine life's invitation. Amen.

Reversals: born again
John 3.1–21
Acts 2.22–24

Under the apple tree I awakened you.
There your mother was in labour with you;
   there she who bore you was in labour.
Set me as a seal upon your heart,
   as a seal upon your arm;
for love is strong as death . . .
Many waters cannot quench love.

(Song of Songs 8.5–7)

[She] forgot me, says the LORD.
Therefore, I will now persuade her,
   and bring her into the wilderness,
   and speak tenderly to her.
          (Hosea 2.13–14)

This reflection is inspired by the occasion of having a young woman tell me her story of coming to faith. She had struggled with addictions for many years, and her gentle trembling, as she unfolded how God had found her, told as much of her struggles as her words. Moreover, she had come to explore with me her sense that God was now calling her to a distinctive ministry. I watched as, before me, the vulnerability of faltering flesh showed mixing with the royalty of divine calling, the palpable power of a brilliant solidity weaving through her God-goldened words as her hands lay quietly shaking in her lap. Despite all her fragility, she was being transfigured before me.

For this is the startling commission: God chooses *me* to belong to him, calls *me* to the honour of serving him. The best ministers I know are those who have, at some stage, been most lost, most without goodness, most distorted, most despairing. When Christ breathes

through these depths, they turn to caverns of crystal, the most cap-
acious holding places for light and darkness. These are people who,
knowing their poverty, and having met it in the dark, are profoundly
available to the life that is God. And they are unafraid, steady, able
to rest at life's fault lines: for Christ has reached all the way down,
has anointed the deepest wounds with the healing oil of resurrection
promise.

Have you allowed your awareness of your brokenness to place limits on your sense of God's presence and action in your life? Have you
considered that your littleness and fragility might become resources
for God's ministry through you?

*   *   *

She sits before me and tells her story. How she found him? Not quite:
more, how he found her. And as she speaks, her light, folded frame is
saying as much as the words she's proclaiming, as her hands make a
trembling circle there in her lap, like a dog's tail curved in nervous-
ness, and her asking, aspiring eyes come leaning at the doors of this
new-found possibility: that where she ends, where all her own gods
have failed, where there is no saving herself from what the trembling testifies, *he starts*. The addictions had meaning, signifying all
those efforts to stun senseless the self's most anguished questions,
to find some peace, some respite. But now, she has discovered him.
And there's more: for the God of this cosmos, the majestic King,
is calling this small, trembling *me* to serve him. She's come to ask
about it, and I'm honoured to behold a creature who – I can tell by
her bearing – has been led out from the desert while holding his
hand.

She still bears her wounds, even as he calls her. She is beautiful, even
as she shakes. As she tells me about coming out of addiction, and
finding this calling to serve him, light is ringing from her eyes. Small
and frail, her body protective-curled, wound up in a caverning chair,
this new source is flashing from her. She is telling me the way by
which she found him . . . This woman has been born again in dark.
She has had the blessing of dying, to her old self. Once swallowed
by the desert of sick self-comprehension, imprisoned by the snaring
darts that snag and hold and pierce, she found that in the hell-place

he was finding her: the one who pours himself into desert so that pressing at what's deepest yields his face.

She has come out limping: this little one who fought with God, and darkness, warring with the elements of self and self's salvation. She has come out of the desert limping, leaning on her lover,[11] hanging on to Christ her brother, having made war with her heart's deepest fears and questions only to discover the Lord who was waiting there to lead her out to freedom.

And we've seen him arrive like this before. For this is how he came, on earth, to those who need a doctor: which is every one of us, of course, as he spends himself out to make and show what kingdom is coming. Just so, his lovers, desert-met, are recognizable, are known, by how the hands that hold the healing, bind and tend and gather and bless, are trembling with the sweetest weakness: by how this serving body limps as fractured earthware even while the Loving's casting cloaks of gold round tiny frames. These are *his* servants' ways, his followers, these kingdom-bringers, heralds cast of light and steel, as delicacy yields, beneath, its granite grounding. The wounds we wear are clothing immortal frames.

Like this searching woman, our transformation may require that we are drawn into deserts, where the very grounds of self are exposed and learn to converse with the God who made them. We come out of the desert – this place of encounter with self and God – limping, for we've discovered that we cannot walk alone. This finite creature cannot source, sustain or ensure her own life. We are utterly dependent. The desert strips us naked to this truth. But, in life's Great Revolution, *now*, even as we limp, we are living strong, for life and death exchange at the Threshing Place where, surrendered to God, the Spirit founds our new and lasting life. Yes, in Christ there is this great exchange, the most vital of our life. Here, death is ousted as defining and bounding all, and life is had by dying from that tired, addicted, fantasy-ridden, self into a life that's full and free and lasting: which is Christ-life.

'Come and die' is our lover's calling and the scandalous call of the gospel, its repugnance to all who insist on being self-made. But there is no loss in any of this, for dying *to our death* is all Christ's meaning. This dying is to lose, to abandon, *unto love* this tortuous work we call our daily living; while what's kept of earthly death is only pregnancy and resting. Such a possibility, such an exchange, requires a genius-move, and it has been achieved, it is finished: Christ's own death outmanoeuvred nothingness, and so we are invited to die *into Christ's death*, whose death was death's overturning. So we die into life as we fall into Christ. The Spirit's gift is to perfect in us our own particular beauteous martyrdom.

We still wear our wounds, as Jesus did risen from the grave. We bear our trembling, in hands or mind or heart. Yet what strikes me, as this woman sits before me, is how she shimmers as Godliness rests and mingles with our frailty.

Questions for reflection

1 Have you allowed your awareness of your brokenness to place limits on your sense of God's presence and action in your life? Have you considered that your littleness and fragility might become resources for God's ministry through you?

2 What 'wounds' do you wear? Have they ever helped you to express and share God's love? *Might* they?

3 St Paul hears Christ say to him, 'My grace is sufficient for you, for my power is made perfect in weakness' (2 Corinthians 12.9). How does God's working with our weakness present a contrast and challenge to the world around you? What are the consequences for the culture in terms of its receptivity to the gospel and the coming of God's kingdom?

4 Raniero Cantalamessa writes that 'The new creation . . . is nothing other than the new birth "from on high" or "of the Holy Spirit" '. 'By the first creation we are God's *creatures*; by the second creation we are also God's *children*.'[12] What does it mean, to you, to be 'born again'?

5 How are the thresholds/events of death and birth and life realigned and redefined through baptism into Christ?

6 Where do you see our culture's woundedness?

7 What sign is there, in the event of our baptism, for the future of the world?

A prayer for today

Lord, it is your genius to have outmanoeuvred Nothingness. As we re-constellate our lives around the shiftings of great signposts, bring us to *live*, in full, embodied consciousness, what we are beginning to grasp in our retuned imaginations. Amen.

Wits' end

John 11.23–27
Hebrews 2.6–9

Subversion. The apparent might of the world is undone, or set to be so, by what's done and to come through a Lamb who is slain and enthroned. For me, the quiet, contesting liturgies of the Easter Vigil and the Ash Wednesday ashing – best when set in night – make the pregnant announcements of a world that is coming to the light. They are subversive in their essence, and all the more so for being ignored by, and unknown to, so many in our culture. 'The meek will inherit the earth.' Who would have imagined *that*? But all kinds of earth-world turnings are set to come.

*   *   *

It's late on Ash Wednesday evening when I gather with a scarce few (never underestimate a remnant, nor its power to testify to half-forgotten mysteries) to take part in an aged and lustrous ritual.

A ritual subversive and unmeaning to a self-assured world.

Within a dead-still space, muted by canvas and turned cavernous by candlelight, arrives the call of the Church, echoing down ancient through the ages, calling the gathered Followers of the Way into the observation, the keeping, of a holy Lent.

Lent.

This time of self-reflection, self-examination, this time to recognize our self-mastered distance from God, to wonder at the mystery of it, so that we might more fully know, experience and comprehend our salvation. The darkness of Lent so that the light of resurrection might mean.

The realization of our fallenness, brokenness, our imprisonment, our selfishness, greed, impatience, envy, our barely concealed preparedness to exploit others so that we might thrive: this sobering realization in order that our deliverance can register in spectacular relief on the tortured landscapes of our lives.

And on this ordinary midweek evening.

At the centre of an act of worship that brings my heart to its knees is the act of ashing itself – the signing of a cross of burnt ash and oil on my forehead, a sign to embarrass both self and world – and those words, 'Remember that you are dust, and to dust you shall return. Turn away from sin and be faithful to Christ.'

I am dust.

Not even the star-dust of some secular consolation, but merely dust.

Particles of earth, naked, without animation.

Destitute dirt.

I am dust.

These words – uttered to me in the midst of life – are more meaningful since I have taken funeral services and pronounced over the dead and waiting, just committed to burial or cremation, that they are 'earth to earth, ashes to ashes, dust to dust'.

Words intimately true, yet a shock to announce every time. Now to hear these words reversed, pronounced over me, in the midst of my living, is scandalous, disgusting, strangely brilliant: a fantasy-shattering pronouncement of my mortality.

I wonder at times like this who was it that began the rumour that the Church is a house of prettified consolations, a system of beliefs premised on the evasion of harsh truths? For I can find nothing more honest and stark and real and uncompromising than the proclamation of what every secular doctrine so ceaselessly and feverishly conceals, in case I should tomorrow stop buying to live: that I will die. Nothing surer. The one thing I do alone: the one thing I with all people do.

I am dust.

And to dust I will return.

Except there's more.

And not because this dust is the dust of broken stars, containing within itself the spark to life, but because an-other exists whose passion will bring me to rise. He will lend me light. I will die. But I will die in sure and certain hope of the resurrection to eternal life. There lies the difference, the incomprehensible, scandalous difference, lodged between the ash-dry cross and the pregnant tomb.

I will rise.

If such seasons bring us, stripped and broken, to stomach-churning truths about the limits of this life, it is only to press our timid souls over otherwise untested horizons, until, as weary pilgrims, we discover not the end of the road, but a new light rising, and rising from the other side, to greet us.

Only at my limit can I see this: only when I have surrendered all efforts to win my life by wit, and instead receive that burnt-ash cross, charred-bark concealing the work of fire, sign of my death and resurrection.

Questions for reflection

1 How do you find yourself responding to this reflection?

2 Where is our culture in danger of distinctly spiritual death?

3 How does our culture meditate on death? What *is* 'death' for our culture? Where do its meditations on this theme occur? (Have you seen films, books, media, advertisements comment on this or make use of the concept recently?)

4 What – precisely – has the New Testament to say to our culture on this theme? Where could this particular component of the gospel get traction on the contemporary imagination? What would it challenge – can you give examples from your recent experience? How could you help to share this good news?

A prayer for today

Lord, help us to believe what is, for us, impossibility: the pregnancy of dust. And for the world around us every day, so often unconsoled, and settled despairing: re-grant, by the presence and movement of your Spirit, a revived aspiration for enduring life. The death of aspiration is itself a wound for healing. Come, Spirit of the living God, and spark the ashes. Show the light the dust conceals. Amen.

Burnt sienna
John 12.1–8

One of my favourite pastimes is to pilgrimage round the make-up counters! It's one small way, within a busy life, to find satisfaction for my creativity. I gaze over the colours of the lipsticks and shadows, and relish the possibility of beauty.

I also notice, though, that these counters are heavily spirit-charged. Once again, the names of the products make claims, either subtly or boldly, for what only a life in Christ can truly give. And what *is* 'beauty'? And why do I long so much to be beheld, and by a gaze that is admiring? Could it be that I *am* so beheld . . .?

*   *   *

I spy the lines from a distance. This spacious heaven-place is brilliantly lit, with counters curved and arabesqued to call the wandering shopper to the chancel. And as I approach the dazzling shelves, all set to shining beneath steely halogens, the rainbow lines of coloured dots announce myriad opportunities to possess, or seduce, to receive power and to wield it. This altar serves (that's 'sells') the sacrament of human power. A sensational red is called 'In Love': it grips me quickly, and already I am rising to the occasion, as I'm warming up, despite myself, to this possibility: the brilliant, heady, frustrated bliss of being in love. This being known, this being desired, this being seen, this feeling much, this splendid lostness in another: Intensity.

'Flat out Red.'

We're at the lipstick counter. And a large cardboard advert calls to me, 'Hey you, you're beautiful.' My seduction has me delayed in noting the irony that what tells me I am beautiful recommends me to the layers of chalks and creams and powder: to cover, and choke, and hide, and enhance, and stimulate my surface to what will be catching fire in you – my little power – though sienna's cast in rawest earth.

Purchase complete, a promise bought, I return to the mall corridors where smoky-eyed models are lining these cathedral walls like sultry angel-sentinels, and one, I notice, has hands aligning high on her thighs in focused offering, is making love to self to sell a dress.

I am assaulted by this raid on what is deepest charged in me.

Because it's yours.

My craving is the clue, this burning out that has me falling deep in love with anyone who smells of you, who owns your fragrance in his skin.

This is how you call me out, your own language stolen for another tongue, your invitation shrunk to what fills bottles, and drops as coloured spots, as promises, on the ends of lipsticks and the plastic cases of shimmer-creams named for enchantment: promised magic. 'Astral dust.' 'Celestial amethyst.' 'Resurrection light.' 'Moon dust.' 'Beloved.' Aspirations to transcendence and immortality.

But we are your people; and you have made us for yourself; and so we burn for you, which is our one way home, our deep-set nature's searchlight. And what would steal this love, this passion, what would bottle and sell this semblance needs a fresh-faced revealing: the magic dustings unlabelled, unsung, and the chemist tinctures draining out to plugholes as false claims to heaven reduce to glinting mica, rusting out the hole.

For the burning is *your* language, your arriving, though (confession) it's our neglect that has us unknowing it. So used we are to being called by word (from being made through Word) – that's well – but we do not know how to translate what comes calling through our guts as well, what sets the ache, as eyeshadows, blushers, concealers, all these paints and ointments conjure with fingers their spells to wake up what's aspiring in us to ethereal, to life-full, to overflow, to dazzling and distinguishing: making us up; making you up; making it up; pretending.

And I remember her, and her impression on that Gospel-writer, writing up her consequence with words of rare sensation: the woman who brings all that perfume, and is breaking it over you. And as she presses roses through your feet, and lends her lips to bless what your death's blessing, I wonder if we're seeing here her scents saved up to call a lover spent on you so that their pouring filling up that house can be love's casting. And I wonder how these beauty shops can come to know what beauty, and its pouring, testifies.

Questions for reflection

1 How do you define 'beauty'? What enhances it?

2 How do you define 'sanctification'? What progresses it?

3 Where have you most recently seen the world attempting to 'sell' what is only God's to give?

4 Think over the past week: where have you seen distinctly spiritual, or spiritually charged, language used to identify a product? How did you respond at the time? How do you feel about your response now?

5 Where are you most tempted? Which labels, signifiers, claims have most power to seduce you? Why? What do these desires reveal to you about how and where God may be speaking to you?

6 'My seduction has me delayed in noting the irony that what tells me I am beautiful recommends me to the layers of chalks and creams and powder.' Where do you notice such paradoxical, or self-contradicting, claims in the culture around you – as it endeavours to secure your love, to entrance your strongest affections?

7 What has the gospel to say to your heart's most vulnerable, most seducible, hope? Does this teach you a wider lesson for ministering to an aching culture – 'culture' which is composed of a matrix of yearnings, promised satisfactions, fears, projections, magnetizers, repellents . . . a complex of desires?

8 How do you understand the relationship between 'becoming beautiful' and 'sanctification'?

A prayer for today

Lord, so much is pretending: and assaults our senses with whispers of your presence. Strengthen in us the gift of discernment, to know what is truly of you, and what pretends. And never for our good only: but that we may help a whole culture to break the spell that confuses its longing, and, in so blurring, obscures both Way and End. Amen.

Constellations
Colossians 1.15–17
Colossians 3.11

———◆———

This poem is in praise of Christ as the one who holds everything together – literally. The genius of it: God sending the One through whom everything was made into flesh to reset that material to right alignment.

*   *   *

Crystal Christ.

Pivot-point of all:
the world's un-wending now Christ-bending
all because you died to set again the pen to Life's designing,
fresh aligning,
by that, mending
what was spending out to Nothingness.

O, glistening lŏgic,
serves destiny by coursing stars along their love-lines first-set
tending,
yet arc-bending back from blank oblivion,
instead to circle light in dawning order.

You are Principle: both morning and the evening star,
sweet axis for all life round which to turn,
yet never to burn
yet ever to burn
besetting entropy
– false prophecy:
hot-set to resurrection
is what's Ending.

Re-constellate!

He's come: the author shaping-out for second-tuning what was
bent,
while cancelling rent
for earth-death, shattered order.

Exquisite logic: spoke and key
is just as much the cornerstone of me!
For You in person come, flesh-blessing,
so to leave the clue
where bodies are Christ-dressing.

I must praise you as the lines of mind receive
a comprehension that brain-lights
as new cohesion spies
that chaos Nothing-ordered dies with night:
while you are holding by your scars
the Everything spilt out with stars
from your own womb: amazing.

And I'm rising: with the ecstasy
of feeling with my thoughts
your cosmos-framing,
hell-thought taming,
heaven-fires naming,
as you crystallize to new refractions
shots of Light and Life: now set to Rise,
for passing through you.

And the mystery now
remaining is that some have minds and knees unbent
to your Reframing
Love: they cannot know you.

True unknowing
is this plunging
into you,
dark space
cloak-circling all.

Questions for reflection

1 What strikes you about this reflection?

2 How do you respond to the statement in the letter to the church in Colossi that Christ 'is before all things, and in him all things hold together?' (Colossians 1.17). Have you meditated on the cosmic significance of this statement?

3 Christ is God as author of order and cohesion in creation. He is a vision of creation's perfect shape. God as Spirit directs the cosmos towards that perfection and, as such, its destiny. Where can you celebrate the coming-to-order which is the world's re-constellation around the person and work of Christ? What does this look like?

4 How does the appreciation of Christ's identity here relate to St Paul's invocation for Christians to be transformed and renewed in their *thinking*? What might an intellectual response to the gospel look like? That is, what might the significance of the gospel be for the life of the intellect?

A prayer for today

Eternal Trinity, we praise you for what is achieved through the Son, as author of Life, and redeemer of what receives new life in him. We pray for this creation in its calling to come to the fullness of manifesting the ordering life of Christ. God, by your Spirit, help us, personally, to re-constellate our lives around the image of the Son, growing evermore into his likeness, and so gaining our freedom. Amen.

Epiphany
Matthew 2.1–12

It's time for some Christmas shopping, and as I search around our nearest shopping centre I discover a small glass ball, filled with glitter, set under lights to enhance the effect, and promising to grant wishes. Here, I see, is the seeking heart of our culture. This little ball would not be produced if there were no hope of its selling: and it *will* sell, to all the many of us who feel the desire for reality to push back when pressed. We are set to enchantment. But can we really buy it? And how do we help the world have the 'epiphany' of realizing what it is often *truly* wishing for? How do we help the world interpret its desires? How do we help people's gaze find, and rest on, the light that is Jesus?

* * *

It's in the knowing.

Quite what generates the light is what our world, exhausted, swirls, evading.

It's a time demanded for buying gifts
so I walk into a shop
where stands a present to be bought:
a clear-shining globe,
full belly pulsing light from millioned starlets
where the managed art-light falls.

Round its neck a label, cordoned,
printed in that speckled-ink of neo-vintage,
aping Home,
s-prays out:
'Star light, Star bright,

the first star I see tonight
I wish I may, I wish I might,
have the wish I wish tonight.'

The little gnostic ball is marked £4.

But where's the pounding light
that bursts with Big-Bang's thrust
to fill out night
not with a Grecian fight as if to say that both remained, distinct,
yet light be winning war?
No: this is the gulping swallow-up of night through
   Light's residing, night be-riding,
      Death o'ertaking only to return and eat the lie

so that: One Star:
the Morning Star,
one light that holds the contours just and speaks his 'constellate'
to every spark that's spat for healing all across the cosmos.

Why would we wish on stars,
their fitful gestures falling fires of origins burnt-out at heart,
when there's to pray to Morning Star
who would our own hearts fire to hearth-blaze homing,
casting far our dreams to what at furthest edges creaming into
darkness speaks as well that all shall live within what lights eternal fires? This man called Jesus.

For he's lighting.

Questions for reflection

1 What do products like this on sale reveal about the beliefs of
the designers and marketers, and the yearnings of the potential
buyers? Can you think of similar examples?

2 If our culture is in need of an epiphany when it comes to recog-
nizing Christ, what would you say this epiphany consists in? How
would you describe it? What needs to be recognized as a star to
follow?

3 In the week just passed, what have been the guiding lights that
you have watched people around you live by – your nearest and

dearest, as well as the stranger and those who walk through the night of an unbaptized culture? As people are making their way through life, what are the signs and markers along the way?

4 What inspires you in this reflection? Through meditation on these reflections, what has become a guiding light for you? Has there been an epiphany?

A prayer for today

Lord, those who are wise come searching for you: they can come 'from the East', from distant lands, yet celebrate the King they now discover. In a culture that aligns stars – signs and wonders – in so many and complex ways for our discerning, hoping to set the routes of our navigation, give us the wisdom to discover and acknowledge where the Christ-light shines: the only star by which we navigate; the only axis, in the night, that leads us to safe harbour. Amen.

Chiselling

All the while, you will grow as you learn to know God better and better.

(Colossians 1.10, NLT)

Sometimes the 'divine sparks' reside simply in the bearing of the person I live with, work with, dance with, worship with . . .

Do you know, or have you known, someone who you feel has a 'holiness' about them? Is there a person of faith whose posture, or character, whose way of being him- or herself, inspires you? It is everyday people – you and me – whom Christ is working in and chiselling, in Spirit, to transform. The saints are the people of everyday – the real, concrete people you work with, see in cafes, pass on trains, meet in nurseries. Who do you aspire to becoming? Who is Christ calling you to be? What you especially admire in others – might this be a clue to your own destiny?

*   *   *

This is in praise of you, becoming creature.

I find myself at a party in the parish. We've not met before, you and I, so there's a certain amount of not knowing where the other's lines reside. And, if I'm honest, it's easy to be defensive these days: you're more likely than not, I fear in myself, to jerk away from the collar and shirt, or to arrive with cascading assumptions.

And then you stump me: apparently, you find even my commitment wan and pale, divided up in altar vows to two great lovers, while with earnest full-heart protest you cry, 'Does no one marry God any more?'

And in this direction you shine: becoming beautiful, as the light that lights you surges to rest at flesh-veil, and you are becoming. As

114

everything you are, which comes from him, begins as floating atoms to re-constellate into the shape that burst out all your being.

You show me Christ: but in your Christening Christ is showing *you*.

And as the author authors through you, not unchanged becomes the page that hosts the lines arriving.

I've seen that in another too, this holiness. The showing is in life's reversing battles: as storming outsides to dead-stilled insides exchange for that glistening peace which is the fruit and mark of silent strivings. Just so, the world mistakes his strength: I see that tenderness, that seeming weakness, oiling out from where, beneath the press of quiet pressures, you've lain down to take upon your little martyrdom.

That tenderness: which in the strength of silent fight reveres the other, permitting the Spirit to chisel the vexed soul concave. Tenderness: which, bearing the strain, dares to permission the impinging, and learns against instinct to dart with you-first longing. Tenderness: which is mingled most exquisite with Godly steel, fusing law and mercy in heavenly alloy.

The clue to who and what is authoring your rewriting is in the basic element of what now flows out from you: this pure, refined and fragranced presence, as still and sure as it is running, mobile, reaching.

Did you know that in this moving you are becoming more yourself than ever? For I see it.

Reaching out for him is chiselling you, as the outstretch of yearning love is making prayer the way by which his spirit comes to master your engraving. And the image that is model, don't forget, is what is beautied human being: you're to be more you than ever as the artist sharpens up, and blends to gold, what's keyed in flesh.

So, then: be radical, ecstatic heart, and shun the lie that claims that Christ is all the flatness that is life without him. And become yourself: so stunning shaped, as all that melts is burning's dross, as all that climbs to life is crowned revival.

Questions for reflection

1 When it comes to an example of following Jesus, who inspires you, and why?

2 If you are in Christ, you are a saint: at peace with God, and an inheritor of his kingdom. What does it mean to you to be a 'saint'?

3 Who do you aspire to becoming in Christ? What do you imagine holiness of life to look like, for you – and those closest to you?

4 'You show me Christ: but in your Christening Christ is showing *you.*' Have you experienced this in an acquaintance?

5 What does the culture around you present as the goal of human *being*: its vision of sanctification? Of human flourishing?

6 Can you think of particular places where a Christian vision of holiness can be *becoming* for those you encounter outside the Church every day?

A prayer for today

Great artist, you behold me with love, tenderness – and aspiration. As I yield to you, come gently to mould and engrave this being, with hands and instruments of love, to my divining. Sometimes, Lord, I relish this awakening. Sometimes, it frightens me: the toils of change seem great. But would you come, and bless the bread that's broken: first, and final author, of my little life. Amen.

Restoration
Matthew 13.31–33

In this reflection, I aim to capture the experience of witnessing a large crumbling house being transformed, over many months, from empty ruin to inhabited home. As I watched the transformation – in both its peaceful and much messier phases (!) – I was struck by the sense of how God similarly works with us.

* * *

Come and walk with me. I'll show you what I've seen over a time: what comes up from ruins.

There is a little village in the Kent countryside with a river and a church and a narrow main street lined with rough-cut cottages, some pale and crumbly as pastel-tinted soft rock. It is a 'well kept' place: fences right-angled, bright white to the sun; lawns carefully curved and patterned-in. Neat-cut windows are cropped with baskets that give each eye an oblong lash – rarely falls a roughly sweeping tendril, something to catch the air. The spirit of this prettiness resides in slumbering tidiness: and many call it 'good', who live for summer.

You and I arrive in autumn, as auburn leaves are crumbling down the tumble trees and lay their beds with yawning.

Now, it's hard for us to see – from the main street – but walking through the heart one day we spy a shadow, deep-pressed back. It is out of light: catching sight only with the impress of distinctive negative, the place where greens dark-down to muddy greys and blend to earth again. Is it only a clearing? No, there is a substance there, we can see, some cave-dwelling mass is bending low, and there's a strange strength posited in how the grey of brick lurks in the spaces

117

between trees. Something is pending, waiting in the earth of autumn's plummy dews.

We cross the street: and as a gateway of a million leaves slow-yields to vision, what was hidden starts to rise and clarify. For we've discovered a house, stretching its dry skeleton of splintered beams towards the sky, and shunting out pale, peeling wings across the dusty earth. There is the memory of order: as testifies the feathering of tight-knit brick, the repeating parallel of gaping frames, once windows. There is evidence of efforts to resuscitate: though rusted scaffolding now merely nets-in the song that tried to rise within the strife. She is a trapped bird, our grounded mass. Her heart lies broken in fractured earthware, in bits of unnameable shale thrown round the yard. These trees are not her homing but her tombing harbour, as she rests collapsed with corporal weight.

Time passes.

And we come again, as much to dust and ashes: though there's come a clamour now. The tomb is no longer resting: neither are the passive streets so slumbering, there are signs of protest through the roads. For the haunt's been visited, and this time there are workers out, and machines hell-thudding, and vans parked crossing the tidy, well-kept highway. Obstruction, reduction, construction all combine to send earth flying, and the house is veiled like some massive ship new-ghosted in a mist-filled harbour. For a time she's invisible, though the strippings of cast-off raiment soar to hit the earth, to ribbon in shroud-like folds.

Time passes.

It is Christmastime. The street is still. But peace has made exchange for slumbering quietude. Bland summer's airs, her flat still gaze, have fled before this sharpness: winter's keen, her black-blue brilliance dividing heady sloth from what comes sparkling. It is night-time, and as all air takes the hue that had back-grounded trees, our house arises sourcing light, herself now lending out the highway's life. And there is laughter, movement, gathering within her walls, new windows giving out what's fresh arrived. And there is fire: at the core a blaze, which lifts and dries and seals and mends the frame that had been caving under gravity's domain. And the fetters, they are unbolted, off; and Order to the walls has clung as bricks replaced are elsewhere cleaned to show the world their working.

And comes nightly, and so tenderly, that flesh-tuned breeze that seeks along the lifelines of the house – this gypsy visitor – to bless the ways into our very breathing.

Questions for reflection

1 Where can you see God in this experience?

The theologian Colin Gunton writes: 'The work of the Spirit is related to the creation's cohesion and destiny in Christ, but his distinct function is at once to restore lost order and . . . transformation into the conditions of the age to come.' He significantly adds, 'This does not happen in a general way, but takes place as particular parts of the creation are set free through Christ and enabled to be themselves, and so anticipations of the universal redemption in the age to come.'[13]

Where have you witnessed 'particular parts of the creation' being 'set free through Christ and enabled to be themselves'?

2 Where can you identify acts of restoration in your own life, or the lives of those you know? What marks out these acts of restoration as being caused by, and orientated to, Christ?

3 Christ is the model of creation's perfection, and the Holy Spirit is the power of – the energy directing – that perfection. For what do you most pray to receive the perfecting work of the Spirit?

A prayer for today

Our Father in heaven, your Son restores life and order – and secures well-being – in particular ways and in particular places. We thank you for Christ, the 'clue' to the nature of this restoration, and the promise of its future arrival in fullness in all ways and places. Lord, we pray that as we receive the one who is the Way, the Truth and the Life, we would evermore see parts of our lives and relationships restored: for our homing in you, and to your glory. Amen.

Fractions

Look around you: and behold the lost. Fractions of Christ's own body, splintered out. Inhabitants of his kingdom, waiting to be brought home. Strangers lingering in the night, before the banquet. When the King returns, he'll bring them in: and how are we as heralds and hosts in the meantime?

I take a visit to a famous London church where the homeless sleep every day in the pews: the dispossessed, the far from home. They are so quiet, slumped invisibly below the pew lines, I do not notice them at first. And then, as I pray silently, and the hum of the city dies down outside, I am alarmed as every nerve in me wakes to the presence of sleeping angels.

*   *   *

I looked for you again today. You were not here: perhaps there was, finally, room at the inn. Your place, the square inlet by the metal gate, spoke of you like people don't, announcing your change of address. No removal lorry is coming to collect what you've left, a buckled cardboard wall and three polystyrene cups. Signs of residence. You may have several, so perhaps I should be specific: it's the place by that phone box, the one with all the girls' first names and grubby digits climbing up the glass. Those inky names call out, even as the phone is silent. They, like your wind-tumbled cups, hinting at hidden worlds from the edge of the Uptown footpath. Tears and groans behind the walls of glass.

As I'm walking, I'm still looking around in case I might catch sight of you – crouched into a corner, pressed into some side-hole or folded up like a discarded embryo, human skin laid bare to rain that lashes.

You are a lost thing, stuffed with bags and cotton wool.

(Christ.)

You are *my* lost thing, stuffed with bags and cotton wool. I wonder where you've gone? Were you a child, bent double there to shield your legs, we'd run to make you know our love. But you *are* a child. Just a grown-up one. We all are.

I was like you, for five minutes, do you remember? And you were shining when they mistook me for homeless with you and pressed pennies to my hand: though while your eyes shimmered laughter I looked down to see how small the coin we dare to give you. They dared to give me.

*

I'm sitting near the back of this famous, splendid church. I close my eyes: sense begins to separate a world now bathed in brown.

Here come the quick-steps, striking bright with single purpose, ringing down the polished aisle.

But further back, as if pressed to the edges – or emerging from beyond what's framed – a sound as deep and slow as the repeated tide weighs over stones with weary dragging weight: these many sleeping angels – who slumber down, invisibly, behind the pews, miraculously able to lie long in wait, unshifting with the flurried flight of passing mortals – snoring.

Eyes opening, I see that one has risen: brought his closed-eye worn-out face, still resting on his hand, to sleep above the pew line. And tourists glide with stunning indifference all through the lines to gather up their pictures: of this marbled surface, this prettied ceiling, that's what their choice will testify. The artifice. And I gaze on that lonely, hiding, sleeping face, and it's like I hear him: 'Why think you I came as a babe? I have something in common with the least and lost of you.' And I see it: you're in the ditch of brokenness, aren't you? I touch you here: I miss you everywhere else, because it's here you're choosing to be, slumbering low, cherishing up what's come to lost though once a mother held him in her arms.

Because you love it all.

*

Out in the street, and in the square, the artists course the edges, dancing out their wild epiphanies. One sets out his protest: rails against the 'selfies', mirroring back with fiery judgement, through his poem, how he sees us screwing Self. And he is fashionless – the prophet ever in, from out of, time – as he cries out for saints, and martyrs, mystics: those who know to see things differently, spark to make the change.

Questions for reflection

1 What struck you about this reflection? What did you notice?
2 Where have you recently been palpably aware of the needs of the world arriving in the landscapes of your daily living? Have you?
3 This reflection was written when powerfully aware of the slumbering presence of gently snoring men like 'sleeping angels' who regularly occupy an exquisite central London church famed for its architecture and music. With an indifference that was vivid in its incongruity, visitors and tourists came to admire and photograph the stucco ceiling while the sleeping angels remained invisible. The listless lostness of the forgotten city lapped up against the impervious centre of crisp, self-contained, busyness, like Christ's own sigh throughout the world.

   Has God called you, recently, to notice forgotten people, forgotten places, sleeping angels? How are you responding?

A prayer for today

Lord, we dare to pray, make us restless for the ones who you are restless for. Give us eyes to see what slumbers at the edges: too hopeless, too abandoned, to crawl into the centre for our gaze. Your dwelling place, Christ who lodges the cross, is clear. Desperation, desolation, are your haunts. Give us the vision to go there too: to host your slumbering angels. To be Christ-bearers. Reconcilers. Amen.

First dance

Then he took a cup, and after giving thanks he gave it to them, saying, 'Drink from it, all of you; for this is my blood of the covenant, which is poured out for many for the forgiveness of sins. I tell you, I will never again drink of this fruit of the vine until that day when I drink it new with you in my Father's kingdom.'

(Matthew 26.27–29)

As a priest, I am invited to attend many weddings. For all their glittering difference, they share a tender hope: the hope that belongs to new beginnings. At one particular wedding, in late summer, as the evening settles in, I am watching the bride and groom seek each other, and I am not only aware that Christ is coming for his bride, but that the whole wedding itself performs, echoes and foretells the cosmic truth: *this world and its Lord have had their first dance.* And that we await a marriage.

* * *

It is purposeful.
It is tentative.
It is passionate.
It is blushing.
It is symbolic.
It is hopeful.
It is specific.
It is pregnant.
It is spreading.
It is meaning.
It is intending.
It is not yet everything.

Falling layers of buttercream lace dress a canopy that, overhead, is studded with stars. Glasses spark with celebration, tables weigh with ribbons and flowers, rising music begins to prophesy that dancing will crown this crystalline day. And sure enough, as the wedding guests pour in, a particular two – a bride and groom – begin to search for one another, knowing what the moment is meaning, and are nearing each another with arms set to embrace as the pressing crowds retreat. Something is destined.

I find, as I watch on from within the crowd, that I am remembering, now, another dance: a dance as historical, as specific in time and place as this, as announced by invitation. It meant the coming together that ever makes this second dancing mean.

It is in the resurrection: for it's here that the Father declares his intention to raise, through the Author and Pattern of Life, and by the creating and renewing power of the Spirit, what is destined for dust to the having of life: to marry earth and heaven.

And this marriage has its feast, I recall, as I survey the lines of pastel-tinted icings approaching the great Wedding Cake. For *that* this wedding cake might mean is caught in the meaning of plain bread and wine: chosen from within the world for pregnancy with Spirit-life by him who pledges to come when we share it in his name. Not iced, or sparkled, or gold-edged, or patterned, or glittered, or embossed, or else-how spun with fantasy, but simply bread and wine to show the marriage of mortality and Eternity co-mingling. It is cause to dance. And so, we dance, though second dancing is bought by this first dance: God's with his world.

And here is that first dance: we see it in that picture, given to us by Jesus himself, of the Father gathering home his Son – Father and Son who have both spent out – as the Son returns home, now towing with him all creation: his bride.

It is first dance: and it pledges. It is first dance: and it promises. It is first dance: and it knows the wedding chamber waits. For this first dance – God's with his awaiting world – professes the marriage, the banquet that is already set.

And in the meantime – God is chaste:

The *Father*'s chastity is this: having given away his son to the world, he accepts that he can only have him back with that cosmos in tow.

And the *Son*'s chastity is this: he has promised never to drink again of the eucharistic vine until it is drunk new *with us* when the marriage is come and creation is home through him.

And the *Spirit*'s chastity is this: he shall ever point to the Christ, to the Son, effacing self, preserving loving's shape and destination.

This whole Trinity: bent in lovers' offering, each one's echoed chastity comprised in being faithful to enact another's homing.

Yes, in the meantime, God is chaste: electing that Freedom should be a betrothal, engaging his world with the brace of a band.

Christ's first dance with us: this is what the world has seen. The wedding bed is yet to be met, where two that live distinct shall, in their being distinct, yet full unite, and so entwine that it's one light that lights the city, all her streets and pathways.

You are invited.

Questions for reflection

1 An event like a wedding announces the coming of God's kingdom resonantly! Can you think of another event or occasion – one you have experienced – that gestures, with similar clarity and power, this announcement, this proclamation?

2 Where else have you seen the world around you resting on the brink of the kingdom's arrival?

3 Are there events or occasions in the culture around you that give opportunities to speak of God's life and being with us?

4 For what are you hoping today?

5 What does Christ's promise – to you, and to the cosmos – mean to you? What do you most look forward to?

A prayer for today

Lord, come! The bridegroom has gone for a little time – and, even with the Spirit, as we wrestle with the pains of this now life, we mourn. And yet we remember that first dance: how you came among us, spoke with us, danced with us, cried with us: healed us, stirred us, chastised us, dazzled us, left us enraptured for one, and but one, lover, ruined for any other.

Your bride, she waits.

And how she longs to clasp the wounded hands that taught her dancing.

Amen. Come, Lord Jesus.

Waiting
John 20.1–11

I am visiting a student in London at the church where he is placed, and have arrived too early. It is only 8 a.m. So I sit on a bench and look at the church: and begin to be caught up in something. The church is a vast Georgian presence, anchored like an aged ship in the early morning mists of expanding city parkland. I run to a cafe and start to write down the words that are landing almost too quickly to capture. It is this deep-fused sense of the Church's silent stalking of Time: her seeming ambiguity and agedness, half-faded in mist, in comparison to the circling city's vivid morning life. And my heart, I find, is pulsing to her hidden song, wishing her out of quietness and that vague, etherealizing purple mist and into the brilliance of final, all-in-all arrival. 'The Spirit and the bride say, "Come."' (Revelation 22.17).

* * *

Early morning travelling, in places yet unvisited,
I feel how you make strange the day,
dew-spangle what you birth –

bricks arranged in unknown sequence:

and this church looms largely from the park
like some beached ship – bulking, rusted, worn and dark –
here stranded, out of time,
and blooms in mauve-grey morning gloom,
leaning, dwelling in expanse
of netted, roseless briars.

And as I feel the pull of love
that can't be had –
that worship – no, *devotion* – at some shrine that feigns of
nearing you –

I know there is another finding to be had:
as Love is righting all love's angles.

This is Magdalene's morning:
morning inauspicious
as the grave-clad garden's misted colour-drained-out wide expanse,
this hanging grey,
that lingers air as tomb.

Yet – sits this sign in pregnancy:
the seeming-sleeper ship
   – *that will awake* –
   Angel of the morning; star of winter gardens caught by night.

Damn it, cannot capture it – how earth swells out
to figure Life's abiding
and Life's rising
in the garden
as the dewy flesh-bed tells
and sweetly testifies
as of that oil that spent itself in blessing
   – to all Life tending –
by the Well; and for the Well.

He is Day-spring
and the freshness tells
what barely this weak pen can strive to tell
but's ceaselessly arranging all the Tides
   – to touch the sides –
      – press out! –
what's bare beholden in the patterns as they stand. For all my
prayers are one:

Would but the Rose explode the day
and well away what hangs in mute suspension.

Questions for reflection

1 Here we are: you, eleventh-hour friend, and I, awaiting a future
that has been won as we rest in what has been won with it, this
'present between the times.'[14] What is the world most waiting
for?

2 Within your own culture, which dimensions of God's kingdom currently remain shrouded in mist? How might you help to dispel this mist?

3 Which aspects of God's life are you particularly equipped to make vivid? Might this be related to the flourishing of your gifts?

A prayer for today

Father, you have raised him – and the stone is rolled away. Because it's rolled, we testify, that love will win, for this we see: that Christ, the clue, has finished it.

And so come, Holy Spirit: and bring what was first love to wedding bed.

And so come, kingdom of heaven: with burst throughout all things as Love is met.

Amen. Come, Lord Jesus.

Pregnant

Revelation 22.17–21

Part of the scandal of the Christian faith – a scandal that often eludes even the imaginations of the faithful – is the everydayness of the ways in which God has revealed himself. The theologian Robert Jenson observes that 'God the Son really has a mother who does not need to be a goddess to achieve this.'[15] Our inherently religious instincts so often have us regressing our view of God out to abstract distances, removing him from death and blood, making him safe, clinicalizing the theatre of theological drama. God cannot really be human, be here, be coming to make a home here with us, be concerned with – have made promises to – this flesh that I am wearing out.

And as I'm sitting on a bus in the middle of the day, one hot summer afternoon, watching a woman caress her heavily pregnant belly with a beautiful, dreamy nonchalance, I'm struck. Our God came just like this before, and he will come just like this again; that is, addressed to the average middle of everyday. Which is not to dilute the extraordinary, but to realize that we have never taken seriously enough, never believed, till then, how extraordinary this ordinary was and is – and shall be. It'll be just another instance of all those stunning reversals to come.

* * *

She's a middle-aged woman; in the middle of the bus; in the middle of the day. And as the bus is rocking side to side, she strokes the bump that swells in primrose-yellow like a sun. And as her downturned eyes absorb the world, her face reflects the light that is beginning at her centre.

It is the most ordinary of afternoons. But this is how he comes: in the stead of day. A woman is the world, and here's the Father's heart adoring what is waiting for its coming. For it's coming: sure as she is rocking side to side what's coming to the day. And it arrives like this: in the middle of this everyday life, in the middle of the bus, in the middle of the day. He is coming.

It *has* come like this: and he is coming, this one who is returned to the Father pregnant with creation. He who births the origin is End: he closes the circle, around the world his wedding band.

> The Spirit and the bride say, 'Come.'
> And let everyone who hears say, 'Come.'
> And let everyone who is thirsty come.
> Let anyone who wishes take the water of life as a gift.[16]

Amen. Come, Lord Jesus. Come Christ, the End and Shape and Light, bent in beckoning out to be your bridge – making your way home.

Questions for reflection

1   What does it mean to you that God's kingdom arrives in the middle of our everyday? Do you see this? Can you help others see this?

2   What does it mean to proclaim to your culture that heaven (God's rule) is coming to earth? That God's vision of our future is not an escape from this earth, but this creation's healing transformation?

3   At the close of these reflections, what do you most want to say?

4   At the close of these reflections, what have you most learned to see? How has your prophetic gaze developed? What do you wish most to share with the culture around you?

A prayer for today

At the close of these reflections, what do you most want to pray?

A *closing invocation*
The agony of prophecy – two temples

———•◆•———

> Then he said to me, 'Mortal, these bones are the whole house of Israel. They say, "Our bones are dried up, and our hope is lost; we are cut off completely."
> Therefore prophesy . . .'
>
> (Ezekiel 37.11–12)

I am at the shopping centre again, our culture's cathedral. As I trawl through a well-known bookshop I'm aware that the self-help section has exploded from its previous corner to overtake the whole floor of the shop. As the number of people suffering from anxiety and depression increases out in the world, the cathedral superstore lays its floor with offerings to Mindfulness, colouring books for adults (a new therapy), *The Ladybird Guide to the Mid-life Crisis*, various texts on aspects of physics (now a religious-spiritual authority), on Randomness, Nothing, Coincidence and Chance: how these explain your experience of life. I weave my way through the heaps of books in a predestined order that has me approaching, consummatively, the altar of transaction, the 'customer collection point', where the till waits to receive our sacrifice for the making of peace with this devastated universe through purchase. Here, behold, the altar frontal, a vast banner, announces in an arabesque of festal colour the shop's central recommendation: 'We love *Reasons to Stay Alive*'; quotation from the key text: 'words, just sometimes, really can set you free' (in case you were in danger of doubting this particular intra-cathedral-chapel's currency).

I pick up the book (there are hundreds of copies stacked right here at the front, and either side of the till: this is meant to be an unmissable offering, the next promised satiation, as you wait to pay) and read the back. This gospel-book's endorsement praises its capacity to show us why and how it might be possible to 'make the most of our time on earth'. It is prescribed as a remedy for depression (written by

132

one who found his way out of this 'pathology'). Though quite how its climactic endorsement evades the despair of that 'illness' which makes us feel 'there is no way back and no way forward' eludes me. It seems strange to celebrate in the presence of this absurdity. I cannot light a candle here. I recall that the nothingness that is the negative manifestation of what we call 'evil' has been described as 'sickness celebrating itself'. I am asked, by this anti-gospel, to dance all the way to my death. This pseudo-release. More books, anyone?

I travel on through the shopping centre, and move through a large department store. We are nearing the end of January, and the large open space is a hotch-potch of mini-landslides, each retailer's section a jumble of tangled clothes under scarlet flags announcing 'SALE': flags like ceiling poppies across a field of carnage, a field strewn with the cast-off hauntings of our culture's obsession with cheap clothes and cash. This aftermath is un-prettified: naked steel frames hold the weeping entrails of discarded spun-plastics like skeletons.

Now we come to a more ordered area (out of 'sale'; we're to re-invest in fresh visions of the Items Just In for the New Season). Beneath the angled halogens, handbags are layered thickly like hung necklaces. This batch, over here, wear a designer label: they fall with plastic surfaces shimmering, glinting mock-gold locks, and hang the air with a clinic tang. And within the display, in the aisle, stands a woman all in black, facing outwards. As I pass, and pause to glance at the bags, she is mute: uncoming. She simply stands, stark, staring, black, in dead-centre of the display that rises like walls on either side of her: preserved. This pale creature is the section's sales assistant.

I am caught by one bag: its design is a neat weave of pink roses over a stark and confused whirling of blacks and greys. The overall effect is disorientating, unnerving. I've seen this design elsewhere, on sta-tionery covers, on clothing: it's a neo-Gothic, neo-Romantic aesthetic that fuses, in its flesh-delicates on deathly void (sometimes it bears skulls), our culture's suspicion that we're playing with contradicting convictions (this move, in consciousness and fashion, came after the resurgence of religious symbolism found on clothes as a tribute to the occult revival in popular TV programmes). I search for the bag's label: to find the script that betokens the creator's intention for me. 'ETHEREAL ROSE – ICON'. I note the absurdity of the price we're paying for plastic. And then consider it's not the plastic we're (ready to be) paying for.

As I walk away, the black-clad priestess remains at the edge of my vision, unmoving. Bored stiff by her job – haunted by the purposelessness of the immediate – she cannot even muster the intention to grasp at the small desire my lingering implied. And I'm suddenly struck by a choice I am making as I walk away and leave her there. I imagine another version of myself – a ghostly alternative to me – who in the moment is peeling away from this real self who is walking off, and, instead, returns to the saleswoman to ask her, as she stands stuck in plastic, steel, death and boredom, has she ever heard of Jesus Christ? And as I imagine myself doing this, I am aware that my feet, my actual, real feet, are instead pelting the glittering cathedral tiles in the opposite direction.

Why do we not say?

Here, in Gethsemane, we have fallen asleep. Our Godless culture has fallen asleep amid the absurdity of its contradicting convictions, stuck in the stasis that is celebrating Nothing at the altars of the Shops. But the Church, also, has fallen asleep: fallen asleep in Gethsemane, passed out with uncertainty and fearfulness in the cramping, listless landscapes of our living day by day, as the Nothing comes from beyond to assault with invisible seeping. And we can't even see it, lost in the transparency of accommodating to what the world is presenting as true, as real. The prophet dies. This present disestablishing, this post-Christendom heave, this post-Constantinian turn, is a blessed rupture, a bending and peeling that sprays off light from deadened planes as the protesting world strains away. It is time to WAKE UP.

On the eighth day (the day after first creation: the first day of recreation) he was named Jesus. The one who saves. Who saves and keeps LIFE. His parents took him to the Temple, as the law required, to present him to God – with thanks, and dedication. A man who had the Spirit living in him felt moved to go to the Temple, and as he entered, found Jesus arriving there. And Simeon, that prophet, announced there and then: here, arriving now, coming now, here, is the hope of the world.

And a woman who was always in the Temple, forever within and imbibing the presence of God, at the exact same time found Simeon, Jesus and his parents. And she beheld Jesus and could not help but overflow with speaking to anyone who came near that here, arriving now, coming now, here, is the hope of the world.

And the prophet said to the little boy's mother, Mary: this child, and the meaning of his life, will disorder the world. He will unsettle the powers. And his presence, his teaching, the enduring significance of his life – and his future – will have the heart of every person seared by the fact of his truth: it will be in relation to *him* that every heart and soul, laid bare, will find and know what is true and real.

And the prophet said to his mother, Mary: and your own soul will be pierced, beautiful one. For not even though, but perhaps because, you kneel to let God come, and be, and fill, and overflow, because you receive him you will know the pain of standing in Gethsemane. His being, his truth, his presence, *is* the *undoing* of the warped and lost, the *cracking* of the staid and held, the *splitting* of the tombed: this freedom, this exodus, comes through the cross that lodges in the death-centre and victories *only as* it death-plumbs what is dead and spent.

He is to die: and she'll be pierced, to watch her own child nailed there. But there's a piercing too for every prophet who stays awake in Gethsemane: who stays awake *to* Gethsemane. For though, by baptism, we can die in his death, and live now raised in his life, so that we never have to come by that cross ourselves: yet, for a world hung in crucifixion – unknowing the lover that has caught and carried it over the canyon that strains life out to Nothing – as we wait in this so particular (and so particularly won) 'present between the times',[17] there is an agony to be stayed awake to: met, acknowledged, spoken to (of Christ and his meaning), and delivered, in prayer, to the healing care of God. Gethsemane contains a universe, a world, a culture, a town, a person, you and me.

It is time for the Church to awake in – to awake *to* – Gethsemane. To wake up and keep watch with the Christ who is making heaven and earth. This is for us to become prophets again: people who, guided by the searing vision of the Spirit, can speak to a culture of its play with death and life; can show back, to a culture, the meanings of its landscapes and its loves; can bring a world to waking consciousness of its clustering round the base of the cross; can speak out those words and actions which constellate the maps and compasses that point cultures, systems and individual people to the One who brings them through the cross – and out the other side.

It's time to let the sparks fly.

*

Then he said to me, 'Mortal, these bones are the whole house of Israel. They say, "Our bones are dried up, and our hope is lost; we are cut off completely." Therefore prophesy, and say to them, Thus says the Lord GOD: I am going to open your graves, and bring you up from your graves, O my people ...'

(Ezekiel 37.11–12)

Notes

1 Kenneth Leech in David Bunch and Angus Ritchie (eds), *Prayer and Prophecy: The Essential Kenneth Leech*, London: Darton, Longman and Todd, 2009, p. 228.

2 Colin Gunton, *Father, Son and Holy Spirit: Essays Toward a Fully Trinitarian Theology*, London: T & T Clark, 2003, p. 87.

3 Evelyn Underhill, *The School of Charity: Meditations on the Christian Creed* and *The Mystery of Sacrifice: A Meditation on the Liturgy*, London: Longmans, Green and Co., 1954, Preface, p. xv.

4 Colin Gunton, *Theology through the Theologians: Selected Essays, 1972–1995*, London: T & T Clark, 2003, p. 121.

5 Acts 17.28.

6 This book is composed within the context of early twenty-first-century culture in the North Atlantic West, specifically, in England. But I hope the questions are so formed as to allow comparable reflections in other cultures also.

7 See the Ordinal for the Ordination of Deacons in the Church of England.

8 For more, see Murdoch's three essays 'The Idea of Perfection', 'The Sovereignty of Good over Other Concepts' and 'On "God" and "Good" ', as collected in Iris Murdoch, *The Sovereignty of Good*, London: Routledge Classics, 2001.

9 See the works of Barbara Brown-Taylor, which wonderfully integrate the earth-life of the body (emotion, affection and passion) in the spiritual response to the arrival of the lover God.

10 Raniero Cantalamessa, *Come, Creator Spirit: Meditations on the Veni Creator*, Collegeville, MN: Liturgical Press, 2008, p. 32.

11 See the Song of Songs 8.5.

12 Cantalamessa, *Come, Creator Spirit*, p. 43.

13 Gunton, *Theology through the Theologians*, p. 121.

14 Karl Barth, *Church Dogmatics I.1: The Doctrine of the Word of God*, London: T & T Clark, 2010, p. 4.

15 Robert Jenson, 'For Us . . . He Was Made Man', in Christopher R. Seitz (ed.), *Nicene Christianity: The Future for a New Ecumenism*, Grand Rapids, MI: Brazos Press, 2001, pp. 75–85 (p. 83).

16 Revelation 22.17.

17 Barth, *Church Dogmatics I.1*, p. 4.

Flo's Story

A little story about prayer

After I was widowed, my daughter Jo persuaded me to go to this tea dance in a church hall, a bus ride away from where I live. It was a way to keep fit and meet a few people and really cheered me up, but I still felt empty inside.

One day Dot, the lady who runs the dances, was handing out these little *Prayers on the Move* booklets, so I took one. I hadn't been to church for years and I hadn't prayed for a long time, but reading this little book, by myself, in my own time, the prayers really spoke to me. I realized what had been missing.

The next week, I told Dot that I'd really enjoyed the book and said I thought it would be nice to go to church. Dot said she'd give me a lift. Now I'm going to church every Sunday, I've found my faith again and I'm so happy. That empty feeling inside has gone away and it's all thanks to a little booklet called *Prayers on the Move*.

Inspired by a true story. Names and places have been changed.

Help us to tell more stories like Flo's. Sign up for the newsletter, buy bags, books and travelcard wallets, and make a donation to help more people like Flo find God through a book. www.prayersonthemove.com.